REFLECTIONS

FOR THE

GRIEVING SOUL

Meditations and Scripture for Finding Hope After Loss

MIKE NAPPA

Zondervan

Reflections for the Grieving Soul

© 2023 Nappaland Communications Inc.

Requests for information should be addressed to:

Zondervan, *3900 Sparks Dr. SE, Grand Rapids, Michigan 49546*

ISBN 978-0-310-46367-2 (audiobook)
ISBN 978-0-310-46366-5 (eBook)
ISBN 978-0-310-46365-8 (HC)

Editor: Kara Mannix

Art direction: Tiffany Forrester

Interior design: Kristen Sasamoto

Cover design: Amanda Hudson / Faceout Studio

Printed in India

23 24 25 26 27 REP 10 9 8 7 6 5 4 3 2 1

It may be the oddest thing I've ever done—looking for this journal and knowing I was looking for a place to write my thoughts and memories—as a last way of capturing them. What do you choose when you're writing the last things? Pink? Flowers? A Bible verse? Well, this is it. And here we go.

—AMY NAPPA

JOURNAL ENTRY, MAY 1, 2016

CONTENTS

INTRODUCTION

After the Funeral

SEPTEMBER 11, 2016, WAS PATRIOT DAY, A NATIONAL DAY to mourn lost heroes.

It was also twenty-three days before my thirtieth wedding anniversary.

And it was the day my wife, *my* hero, breathed one long, final breath and then departed this world for better shores. Cancer took my girl's body after a bruising, no-holds-barred, thirteen-month battle, and—

Maybe I'm getting ahead of myself.

For almost three decades I was married to the woman of my dreams. Her name was Amy. I think you would've liked Amy. Actually, you would've loved her. Everybody did.

When it was evident that Amy was in her last days, people came from all over the world for just a few final moments with her. They called her, begged for her to call them, trekked across nations and states to visit her hospice room in Colorado. They texted, emailed, sent cards, and more. I finally wanted to just tell them all to stop . . . but Amy wouldn't let me.

"Mike," she told me gently, "we have to remember that my death isn't about me." (Yes, she really said that.) "People need a chance to say goodbye, and we need to give it to them. Whoever wants to come, let them come. Just plan it so they don't come all at once."

So I made a schedule and arranged visits, and I made sure to keep plenty of boxes of tissues nearby.

And they came, and everyone had stories to tell about how my girl had changed their lives—how she had loved them, encouraged them, made them laugh, shined God's light into their lives, made them feel valued, drawn them closer to Jesus.

There was just something about Amy. She was everyone's best friend and no one's enemy.

About ten or eleven days before she traded the pain of this world for the fullness of joy, a friend visited us in our home. As Amy lay in her bed, exhausted, ready to pass out again, the friend said, "I hope you know how much I love you."

A soft smile touched Amy's lips. "I do," she said, eyes closed, already drifting into dreamland. "I feel very loved.

By everyone." A peaceful breath passed, and she sighed again into the room, "I feel very loved."

And then September 11, 2016, came around. I was sleeping in a cot next to her hospital bed. I woke up at 1:18 a.m. and checked on her—she was still living. I tried to go back to sleep, but I couldn't. At 1:28 a.m. I heard a long, sustained breath flutter and hum through her vocal cords— and then nothing more. By 1:33 a.m. I knew she was gone.

I thought I was ready for that moment. I mean, by the time she stopped breathing, I'd been praying for God to take her, to show His mercy, to end her pain once and for all.

You see, my girl suffered.

And there was nothing I could do about it, so I suffered too. A different kind of suffering, but pain nonetheless. For weeks I'd prayed for God's mercy to come. I'd spent nearly a year in what the medical professionals called "anticipatory grieving." But nothing had prepared me for the absolute devastation of life without my girl.

I am still unprepared for that.

After she died, after the funeral, after weeks of relentless sorrow, I finally begged our friends for help.

"I'm looking for a hundred scriptures to encourage me while I trudge lead-footed through this awful, (seemingly) never-ending time of sorrow," I posted on Facebook. "I'd like to print them out and read a new one each day, all day, for one hundred days. Will you share your favorites with me?"

And they did.

I also found scriptures from Amy herself, left behind for me in the green journal she kept in the months before she died. And I added a few of my own favorites as well. I collected them all, printed them on cards, and kept those cards always close by me.

I have drunk from that well of Scripture every day since, reading my cards several times a day, sometimes journaling my thoughts, sometimes praying God's Word aloud . . . sometimes just crying as I read because I don't have the strength to do anything more.

During those first hundred days after the funeral, there was one day when I sat in a grief-support group, weeping, watching, and listening to the pain of others like me. I said to the Lord, "Somebody needs to do something to help these people. To help people like me." In that moment Jesus seemed to whisper, "Maybe 'somebody' is you."

And so, a few terrible months later, I took one hundred of my Scripture cards and organized them so I could share them with somebody who was heartbroken. Somebody like me. Somebody like you.

Somebody facing life . . . after the funeral.

At first these collections of scripture were held in one hundred envelopes. I gave them to friends (too many friends) who faced the loss of someone they deeply loved. "Open the first envelope on the day of the funeral," I said. "If it helps, keep opening one envelope a day until you run out. Maybe sometime over the next one hundred days, something in here will be grace enough for that moment when you need it."

Then I found I couldn't keep up with all the printing and cutting and enveloping, so I did the next best thing and put them into this book, which I wrote over the course of the first year I spent without Amy beside me. I added some forty reflections from my private journaling—prayers, really. Grief poured into my computer keyboard. I called out to God in response to His Word, just Him and me having honest conversations. By the end of that year, this book was ready to share . . . but I wasn't ready to let it go. Not yet. I put the whole thing into a "someday" file on my laptop and, honestly, eventually, forgot about it.

Five years later, in 2022, my friend Neal passed away. I watched from a distance as his new widow and their beautiful daughters struggled with unfathomable grief after the funeral. Again I heard Jesus whisper, "Maybe 'somebody' is you."

So here we are now, this book finally out of its purgatory on my laptop and into your hands. I hope it gives you enough grace for this moment.

Once, not long before she died, Amy woke up and called my name. When I went over to her, she clutched my hand

and whispered, "I was dreaming about you. I was dreaming that you were changing the world."

"OK," I joked. "I'll get to work on that."

She smiled, nodded, and drifted away again.

I don't know that I will ever actually change this world—I kind of doubt it, really. But I do know that if you're reading this book, your world has been irrevocably changed by the death of someone you love.

I'm sorry. I'm so, so sorry.

You are in an awful time. And you deserve help as you grieve.

Right now is unbearable, I know. Forget about "one day at a time," right? Let's shoot for "the next ten minutes" and see how that goes. That's why this book exists. For you, for me, for the next ten minutes.

So this is my prayer for you now, after the funeral:

May God be noticeably near to you. May the promises and pains of His Word comfort you today as they did for me yesterday. And may they give us both the strength we need to wake up and face tomorrow. Or at least the next ten minutes.

With love to you, my new friend,

MIKE

DROWNING

I am an overdue library book waiting to be returned to its rightful Owner.

—AMY NAPPA

JOURNAL ENTRY, MAY 4, 2016

Have mercy on me, LORD, for I am in distress.
Tears blur my eyes. My body and soul are
withering away. I am dying from grief; my years
are shortened by sadness. Sin has drained my
strength; I am wasting away from within.

PSALM 31:9–10 NLT

THIS IS WHAT GRIEF FEELS LIKE . . .

A constant, dull ache behind the eyes, like a headache just forming or finally going away.

Raw, red skin underneath the nose from crying and wiping tears.

A dense, faint, frightful ringing in the ears that backgrounds every conversation, every waking moment.

A perpetual, dry tastelessness in the mouth, no matter what foods are eaten.

A soft, clammy coldness in the skin that just desires to feel safe but doesn't, no matter how often it's touched.

A dull, hungry feeling in the stomach that isn't hunger because, well, you just don't feel like eating, but that burning goes on inside you anyway.

The never-ceasing smell of your own fear, of your own sweat, of your own unending despair.

Frequent tightness around the heart muscle, something no amount of stretching loosens.

Recurring moments, a dozen times a day, when you think you might be having a panic attack, only to be disappointed and find that, no, you are just living, and maybe this is going to be what that's like from now on.

Relentless exhaustion from lack of sleep and constant sorrow.

Complete, absolute, total, unforgiving helplessness.

The nagging feeling that it's all really your fault, that there must have been something, anything you could have done to save her.

Dying, without death to end your pain.

Ah, Jesus. Jesus. Jesus . . .

Have mercy on me, Lord. I am in distress. Like David of old, I'm wasting away from within.

Please have mercy . . .

PRAYER FOR TODAY

Lord Jesus, sorrow feels inescapable for me. So if I must grieve, then help me to do it well—to the fullest, to the utmost, into Your arms.

Amen.

> I have set the LORD always before me;
> because he is at my right hand, I shall not be
> shaken.

PSALM 16:8 ESV

I HEAR HER VOICE STILL, MURMURING PSALM 16:8 TO herself, to me, to anyone who listened. It was her favorite scripture—but You know that, Lord. She must've whispered it to You a thousand times, rote in her mind but always fresh in her heart.

"I have set the Lord always before me . . . ."

How I wish I could do that now, the way she did. I want to rest in the words of the Psalmist the way she rested in them all through chemotherapy. Through setbacks and broken hopes and hearts. Through pain and weariness. Through goodbyes and tears.

"I have set the Lord . . ."

I dreamed of Amy last night, Jesus. At least I think it was a dream.

We stood in a simple space, clean and free. Somehow in that thin place my girl both had cancer and yet had never had cancer. I can't explain it; I won't try. On a table between us was a letter, one page. More of a note, really, than a letter. Amy smiled at me. I wanted to reach out and hold her, just breathe in her warmth again, but she pointed to the letter on the table.

"Mike Nappa!" it said in her handwriting. "You know you are loved!"

And then I was alone in my bed, sleeping on the right side. She was no longer there to take up the space on the left. In the darkness I wondered to myself, *How can I know I am loved anymore? How can I ever know love now that she is gone?*

I have set the Lord always before me . . . He is at my right hand . . . I shall not be shaken.

She used to whisper those words in the nighttime. They comforted her. She trusted them all the way to the end.

It is nighttime again in this lonely, empty house.

Lord, I hope those words are still true.

PRAYER FOR TODAY

God, I set You before me now, in my thoughts and in my heart. Even as my body shakes with tears, do not let my soul be shaken.

Amen.

This I declare about the LORD: he alone is my refuge, my place of safety; he is my God, and I trust him.

PSALM 91:2 NLT

He heals the brokenhearted and binds up their wounds.

PSALM 147:3 NIV

He was despised and rejected—a man of sorrows, acquainted with deepest grief. We turned our backs on him and looked the other way. He was despised, and we did not care. Yet it was our weaknesses he carried; it was our sorrows that weighed him down.

ISAIAH 53:3–4 NLT

You number my wanderings; put my tears into Your bottle; are they not in Your book? When I cry out to You, then my enemies will turn back; this I know, because God is for me.

PSALM 56:8–9 NKJV

LOOK AT THIS, LORD.

Jeanne has come over and left me a gift on the front porch. I think there must be either thirty-six or forty-eight bottles of water in this giant, shrink-wrapped pack. I'm so dehydrated, I may need them all.

I never knew I had so many tears inside me. I never realized you could keep crying even after dehydration set in, or that you could still cry and not shed even one tear while doing it.

I wonder if You really are keeping my tears in Your bottle. Or is that just a little poetry from an ancient songsmith?

It must be messy if You do keep these tears.

Thirteen months is such a long time to cry. I spent the

first eight months crying and trying to help my girl live, and the last five months sobbing and trying to help her die. I feel like I should be all cried out by now, but I know I'll never stop weeping. Even when my eyes dry up and these water bottles are all gone, there will still be tears flowing inside me. I think You know what I mean.

For months before she died, Amy kept quoting the last part of Psalm 56:9 to me. "God is *for* you, Mikey," she'd say. "No matter what happens, God is for both of us."

I'm having trouble believing that right now. I'm worried that maybe You are now against me, and if You are, I am worse than lost.

Today I walked through every room in this desolate house. I took my time. I stepped slowly, as if walking on hallowed ground, spreading my sorrow into every empty space. I found You waiting, Jesus, in every single room, in every tiny closet. I know You are here with me . . . but for the first time in my life, I don't feel any comfort from having You near.

Why is that? Why won't You hold me like You've held me before? Why are You here but pulling away from my pain?

I know, I know. Things are not what they seem. You are here, and if You're letting me suffer, it is because You are suffering alongside me. I long for Amy, and in her absence I'm desperate for Your Spirit to come and ease this pain.

Your Spirit is near. I know this both physically and instinctively. I need Your Spirit.

Tonight I will close my eyes and wait for You to come and bring comfort to my soul. I will wait because . . .

Because God is *for* me.

Keep me safe, my God, for in you I take refuge.

PSALM 16:1 NIV

LORD, YOU KNOW MY FRIEND ERIC. PLEASE BLESS HIM somehow today.

I still remember the look on Amy's face when I first played Eric's song for her, when she realized he'd taken her treasured Psalm 16 and created a gift of music out of it. "That's, that's . . . my psalm," she'd said from her bed. And she started weeping and laughing at the same time. "He made a song for me from my psalm!"

Well, it was actually a song to begin with, but I didn't say that, and I was crying sad-happy tears too. I hugged her instead, and we listened to Eric's song and cried and smiled. She loved his gift. It was precious to her.

And now I'm hearing it again, listening to the haunting beauty and peaceful worship wrapped up in Eric's voice and guitar. It is beautiful.

Keep me safe. *Oh God, keep me safe.*

I didn't understand how much of my safety was wrapped up in that tiny little woman You gave me as my wife. I feel naked and afraid now.

I'm not used to being afraid.

I don't remember ever being afraid, not really, not like this. My doctor has called it "clinical anxiety, a grief response." I just know I feel fear like I've not experienced before.

In You I take refuge.

Lord, please bless my friend Eric today. I felt just a bit of Your refuge, Your safety, in the melody of his song. It was nice to have relief, even temporarily, from the constant fear that creeps inside and through me.

PRAYER FOR TODAY

Keep me safe. *Oh God, keep me safe.* I don't even know what that looks like, not really. All I can do now is trust You and pray these words: Oh Jesus, please keep me safe.

Amen.

LORD, listen and be gracious to me; LORD, be my helper.

PSALM 30:10 HCSB

Precious in the sight of the LORD is the death of his faithful servants.

PSALM 116:15 NIV

The LORD is good, a refuge in times of trouble.
He cares for those who trust in him.

NAHUM 1:7 NIV

———

Because he bends down to listen, I will pray as
long as I have breath!

PSALM 116:2 NLT

> Blessed are those who mourn, for they will
> be comforted.
>
> MATTHEW 5:4 NET

JESUS, WHAT AN ODD PROMISE YOU'VE MADE HERE.

I mourn today, just like I did yesterday, just as I will tomorrow. I can do nothing else, despite my best intentions. So why don't I feel blessed?

I know the history. I've seen the dictionaries. I know that the word "blessed" meant "happy"—or in literal Hebrew, "How happy!"—when You said it. The Greek equivalent that Matthew wrote down is *makarios*, a heavenly "state of happiness and well-being." So Your promise in Matthew 5:4 could be interpreted, "How happy are those who are sad!"[1]

That makes very little sense to me right now.

I will dig deeper.

It appears that *makarios* carries many shades of meaning. It actually implies that one is "lucky," not so much in the sense of random luck, but in the sense that You orchestrate seemingly random—even devastating—events to deliver happiness in a person's life. And, strangely, it is a congratulatory term, as in, "Congratulations for being chosen to endure sorrow!"[2]

Hmm. If this is true, then even in the worst of circumstances . . . even when my wife has died painfully from cancer . . . I can still find a way to be happy?

Funny, that's exactly what she told me to do. "After I'm gone, don't close up this house and hide away from the world. Open the curtains. Let the sunshine in. Find a way to be happy."

I do not yet understand this. My soul hurts with what feels like impenetrable anguish. And yet, Jesus, You have promised me blessing in this pain. So today I ask You to keep Your Word.

I mourn today, Jesus. I can do nothing else.

Please keep Your promise and *makarios* all over me today.

PRAYER FOR TODAY

Jesus, teach me personally, intimately, how blessing works. Open my curtains, and let Your sunshine in. For just a few minutes today, help me find a way to be happy.

Amen.

My tears flow endlessly; they will not stop until
the LORD looks down from heaven and sees.
LAMENTATIONS 3:49–50 NLT

In the same way the Spirit also joins to help in our weakness, because we do not know what to pray for as we should, but the Spirit Himself intercedes for us with unspoken groanings.

ROMANS 8:26 HCSB

The cords of death entangled me, the anguish of the grave came over me; I was overcome by distress and sorrow. Then I called on the name of the LORD: "LORD, save me!" The LORD is gracious and righteous; our God is full of compassion.

PSALM 116:3–5 NIV

> My soul melts from heaviness; strengthen
> me according to Your word.
>
> PSALM 119:28 NKJV

TOMORROW WOULD'VE BEEN MY THIRTIETH WEDDING anniversary with Amy. Before cancer, we had planned to have a big party to celebrate this date—to rent a hotel ballroom, invite all our friends, hire a DJ, get dressed up, and spend the evening dancing and laughing and loving each other again.

Cancer changed those plans.

Visiting this anniversary date without Amy makes me intensely sad. (I actually feel like throwing up whenever I think about it.) I think I should do something tomorrow that will make me happy instead of locking myself in my room and being sad all day long.

But I know I won't.

Sigh.

My soul melts from heaviness, Jesus. Will You strengthen me? Or is that promise just for somebody else?

I guess I'm about to find out. Tomorrow.

PRAYER FOR TODAY

I am weak, Lord, so You're going to have to be strong for me today. I think that's just the way You like it anyway. And it's how I need it. So thank You.

Amen.

I will lift up my eyes to the mountains; from where shall my help come? My help comes from the LORD, who made heaven and earth. He will not allow your foot to slip; He who keeps you will not slumber. Behold, He who keeps Israel will neither slumber nor sleep.

PSALM 121:1–4 NASB

The Lord is my light and my salvation—so why should I be afraid?

Cast your burden upon the LORD and He
will sustain you; He will never allow the
righteous to be shaken.

PSALM 55:22 NASB

LAST WEEK, QUITE BY ACCIDENT, I DISCOVERED TWO OF
Amy's journals. I was looking in her wardrobe and noticed
that one of her shirts had fallen to the floor. When I went
in to pick it up, I found the journals—plus some gifts she'd
tucked away for our nieces, way too many bottles of lotion,
and various other small items she'd taken to storing on her
closet floor.

One book is dated from March 2008 to May 2015,
ending just before the cancer diagnosis. It was a "dream
journal" given to her by a friend, and for seven years she
kept a record of her thoughts and dreams and questions
about faith and life in it.

She switched to a Mickey Mouse journal on August 18,
2015, the night before the first cancer surgery. There's
only one entry in that journal, several pages long, of all
her thoughts and fears and faith and a few Bible verses,

written as she faced for the first time what she knew might be the end of her life. She didn't write like that again until May 2016, when she bought a green journal in which she wrote letters to her loved ones in the months before she died.

These journals are now my most precious possessions. My girl was known as this bright, outgoing, creative soul (and she was!), but her journals reveal an Amy most people never saw—a thoughtful, reflective, intelligent, insightful woman who wrestled deeply with sorrows and faith and truth and life—yet who always found joy in simple treasures like family and friends and Scripture (wow, she loved the Psalms!) and, yes, faith and love.

When she was dying, so many people told me how much they admired Amy's great faith. I think, after looking through her journals, what they admired was not "great faith" but "the same faith." Apparently she'd learned well the lesson of Psalm 55:22.

Amy's perspective on God and life, her constant pursuit of intimacy with Jesus, her desire to be His instrument—those things all stayed the same in the spotlighted days of death as they were in the obscure years of life that came before. Amy's great faith was really just everyday faith, unexpectedly put on display in her hospital bed.

In one of her hardest moments, she wrote: "Rough and honest conversation with the doctor—not good news. But in spite of that—I am loved, by God, by my family, by so many friends. I want to live, but I know that no matter what, I am in God's hands."

This was normal for her, to say simply, "I am in God's hands." She used to hold out her palm, spread her fingers as if letting worries spill through them like water, and say those five words to me. She knew them to be true.

Lord Jesus, I watched Amy cast her burden on You as she was dying. I witnessed it firsthand as You sustained her through it all. What I didn't realize was that, even in her weakness and pain, *she* was also sustaining *me*. I leaned so heavily on her.

I'm falling now, Lord, falling hard. I want to cast my awful burden onto You like she did, but my arms don't have strength enough to lift themselves, let alone cast anything onto anyone. So help me, please. Do the casting for me, so You can sustain me while I am so weak.

Like you did for Amy.

PRAYER FOR TODAY

Holy Father, in spite of everything, I am loved by You. I call on Your love now and say: *I am in Your hands.*

Amen.

I can never escape from your Spirit! I can never get away from your presence! If I go up to heaven, you are there; if I go down to the grave, you are there. If I ride the wings of the morning, if I dwell by the farthest oceans, even there your hand will guide me, and your strength will support me.

PSALM 139:7–10 NLT

Good people pass away; the godly often die before their time. But no one seems to care or wonder why. No one seems to understand that God is protecting them from the evil to come. For those who follow godly paths will rest in peace when they die.

ISAIAH 57:1–2 NLT

I will lead the blind by ways they have not known, along unfamiliar paths I will guide them; I will turn the darkness into light before them and make the rough places smooth. These are the things I will do; I will not forsake them.

ISAIAH 42:16 NIV

The Spirit of the LORD God is upon Me because the LORD has anointed Me to preach good tidings to the poor; He has sent Me to heal the brokenhearted, to proclaim liberty to the captives, and the opening of the prison to those who are bound . . . to comfort all who mourn.

ISAIAH 61:1–2 NKJV

You will make known to me the path of life;
in Your presence is fullness of joy; in Your
right hand there are pleasures forever.

PSALM 16:11 NASB

THE CHAIR NEXT TO AMY'S HOSPICE BED WAS ONE WE
called "the hand-holding seat."

During that last week of her life, my girl lay in a coma,
growing colder by the hour, waiting to be released from
her nonresponsive body and welcomed into Jesus' heaven. I
spent hours in that chair, wanting nothing more out of my
life than to hold her hand while it was still warm.

On her last night, I sat in that lonely chair, holding her
hand, and found a Gideons Bible stored in the end table in
front of me. So I turned to Amy's favorite psalm and read
it aloud to her. I finished with the words, "In Your presence
is fullness of joy; in Your right hand there are pleasures
forever."

Amy and I used to talk about heaven in the years
before she was sick. What would it be like? What did it
hold? And one day as we were talking, I said to her, "What

I'm looking forward to most about heaven is just that Jesus is there." She thought about that for a moment, then nodded and smiled. After that, whenever anybody asked her about heaven, she'd say, "I don't really know what it'll be like, but I do know the best thing about heaven: Jesus is there."

During the last days before her coma, Amy would sleep for long hours, then wake up briefly. Sometimes she'd sigh when she woke up. "Why am I still here?" she said to me more than once. "I'm ready to go. I'm ready to be with Jesus."

Once I came into her room and found her in the closet, digging inside a dresser drawer with a hanger. "Honey," I said, "what are you doing? You need to go back to bed."

"I just thought I'd work in the garden for a little bit," she said.

"There's no garden in the closet," I said, confused. "Now, come on, let's go back to bed."

She went agreeably, and when she was settled in bed, she looked up at me. "First of all," she said, "there *is* a garden in the closet. But"—she held up a hand to keep me from interrupting—"we can discuss it later." Then she changed the subject, and we chatted for a while until she was ready to go back to sleep.

In Your presence is fullness of joy . . .

I wonder now if there really was a garden in the closet,

if maybe Jesus was giving Amy a glimpse of what He had prepared for her, of some glory that was to come.

In Your right hand there are pleasures forever.

Lord Jesus, I miss holding my girl's hand. So. Much.

But when her fingers fell from mine, I'm glad You were there to take her hand . . . to embrace her . . . to welcome her once and for all into the fullness of Your joy.

She was looking forward to that.

PRAYER FOR TODAY

Precious Lord, take my hand . . .

Amen.

I look for your deliverance, LORD.

GENESIS 49:18 NIV

KICKING

Tony, will you please keep an eye on your dad? I know he'll say, "I'm fine," but it's a bunch of crap. He needs you. . . . I'm serious. He needs you.

—AMY NAPPA

JOURNAL ENTRY, MAY 18, 2016

Don't leave me all alone, LORD! Please, my
God, don't be far from me! Come quickly
and help me, my Lord, my salvation!

PSALM 38:21–22 CEB

TODAY MY SON TOOK ME OUT TO SEE A MOVIE. WE HUNG
out like old times. It was good.

My son's a great person, and I'm grateful for his friend-
ship now that he's an adult with a family of his own. And
yet . . .

The whole time we were together I could barely hold
back my grief, and then as we left the theater, it just came
out of me in spite of my best efforts. We had to wait until
my eyes cleared of tears before I trusted myself to drive out
of the parking lot.

Tony was patient with me and afterward insisted I
hang out at his house a little while instead of just dropping
him off. (See, I told you he's a great guy.) So I did, which
was also good.

When I finally got home, I sat down and wrote a long
Facebook post about what I'm learning of grief . . . then I

actually read it and realized it was just more of me weeping into my keyboard. Again. (That gets so tiring. Even I'm sick of reading that maudlin stuff.) So I put it in my "too bleak for sharing" file, and now I'm just going to share with you the end of it, if that's OK:

I think I will be broken for a while.

I'm sorry.

PRAYER FOR TODAY

Lord, I think I will be broken for a while. Please don't be far from me, but come quickly and help—especially today.

Amen.

In panic I cried out, "I am cut off from the
LORD!" But you heard my cry for mercy and
answered my call for help.

PSALM 31:22 NLT

MY DOCTOR HAS RECOMMENDED THAT I SEE A CLINICAL
psychologist for help with severe depression, which is fine,
except that every time I go to see her she's required by law
to ask me the same three questions:

1. "Have you had thoughts of hurting yourself or
   others?" (Well, I'd like to smack the person who
   makes you ask me these same questions week
   after week.)
2. "Have you planned your own suicide?" (If I had,
   do you really think I'd tell you?)
3. "Do you know the number to call if you need
   help?" (I guess 911 is hard for some to memorize?)

But really, it's OK, Lord. She only wants to help me,
and I think, sometimes, she really is concerned about me.

She's paid to care, I know, to listen, to offer encouragement, but there are moments when I see her eyes mist with tears to match mine, when silence fills the room because, it seems, she just doesn't know what to say to make me feel better. For some reason, that makes me feel better.

Today she asked me about You. She wanted to know how You and I are gettin' on now that Amy is dead. "It's normal to question your faith or be angry at God after the death of a loved one," she said.

So I thought about it for a minute.

Was I angry at You? No. Not at all, actually. How could I be angry at the only Person who gives real hope of comfort in these awful days? That'd be like cursing the firefighter who's come to deliver me from a burning house. Am I questioning my faith in You because Amy died? Well, first I'd have to question why I expected either Amy or me to be granted an exemption from death. I've known my whole married life that one of us would die first and leave the other behind. My wedding vows did include "till death do you part," after all. I always just expected it would be me to go first.

But I digress.

So how are You and I gettin' on, God?

Sometimes I feel a lot like King David of old—panicky, wondering if maybe I'm cut off, if You've turned Your face away from me. In a way, as awful as that would be, it'd also be something of a relief. If I could convince myself to believe that lie, then I could blame You for my sorrow, maybe even be angry at You and all that other stuff.

But no matter where I turn, no matter how hard I kick or how loud I scream or curse or cry, still, I sense You nearby. I know You are here, with me, even though You are letting me suffer. My question to You is not why I have such debilitating grief, but how long I must keep this pain in my soul.

How long, Lord? I guess, like David, all I can do is pray:

> Lord, hear my cry for mercy.
> Jesus, please, answer my cry for help.

P.S. (1) No, I haven't had thoughts of harming myself or others. (2) No, I haven't planned my own suicide. (3) Yes, I know the number to 911.

PRAYER FOR TODAY

How are You and I gettin' on, God? Please don't cut me off. Please hear my cry for mercy and answer my cry for help.

Amen.

Oh, I must find rest in God only, because my hope comes from him! Only God is my rock and my salvation—my stronghold!—I will not be shaken. My deliverance and glory depend on God. God is my strong rock. My refuge is in God.

PSALM 62:5–7 CEB

May your unfailing love be with us, LORD, even as we put our hope in you.

PSALM 33:22 NIV

> He gives power to the weak, and to those
> who have no might He increases strength.
>
> ISAIAH 40:29 NKJV

MY SOUL FEELS GRAY AND GAUNT TODAY, AS IF WIN-
tered by sorrow and weakened by age. I think a good fall
would break it into unmendable pieces, like Humpty after
the wall. But I forget, this brittle, invisible thing is already
broken. Maybe that's why it never stops throbbing, light
or dark, summer or winter. I fear I will always be broken,
and I must learn to walk with a limp. It is a hard thing to
learn alone.

I used to lean on her in times like this.

Now I just lean into the empty grayness and surprise
myself with the fact that I'm still standing. Yet I stand
nonetheless. Broken things, I think, must be stronger than
I once believed.

Maybe this is why God allows a soul to gray with
heartbreak, to crack and splinter under the aging weight
of sorrow until . . . well, until something I don't know yet
happens, something I can't imagine or describe. Maybe

that's what's happening to me now. Maybe the old prophet was right, and when I am weak, You make me strong..

Be strong today, Lord, for I am weak in every part of me.

I am so weak.

PRAYER FOR TODAY

All right, Jesus, here's Your chance to prove Your Word is true. You give power to the weak. Guess what? I am very weak. I'm ready for Your strength.

Amen.

> I will praise the LORD at all times; my mouth
> will continually praise him.
>
> PSALM 34:1 NET

AMY DIED ON A SUNDAY. SHE SPENT THE LAST WEEK OF her earthly life in a coma, sometimes groaning, sometimes crying, never opening her eyes, unable to move or speak.

It was awful, Jesus. You know. You were there.

On the Friday before her death, I had Amy's favorite worship music playing near her hospital bed. It was just You, me, and Amy in the hospice room. And Kalley Heiligenthal of Bethel Music singing "Ever Be" softly over my tinny little speaker.

I wonder, *Can I sing this worship song, right here, right now, in this heartbreaking place? Do I have it in me to promise God that I will continually praise Him, no matter what?*

I opened my mouth, and a dry, cracking sound came out. I looked at Amy, already more gone than here. My throat constricted, and I started weeping (again).

She was so small, my girl.

But Kalley Heiligenthal kept singing, so I tried again.

"Your praise will ever be on my lips," I rasped through tears. *Not good enough*, I told myself. *Either you mean it, or you don't. Make up your mind.*

So I swallowed once, twice, and opened my mouth again.

The words came out right that time.

I won't say they were strong or loud (because You know; You were there), but they were firm. I could tell I meant them. In that moment, a moment worse than I could ever imagine, King David's words were still true for me.

I will praise the Lord at all *times . . . .*

I discovered later that David wrote those words while in enemy territory, in a place where his life was in imminent danger. Apparently his situation was so desperate that he had to pretend to be insane in order to escape . . . [3] and still he sang praise to God.

I'm going to be honest. My singing praise to Jesus in that moment didn't help me feel better. When I was done, sorrow still filled my soul like a dirty glass spilling ugly water inside all of me. But it was important for me to look at the woman I loved most in this world, the thing I loved more than my own body—the person I'd loved for longer than I could remember—to watch my own life dying within her tiny frame and to know that even then, even there, I could still remember that God is good.

God is always good.

So, Lord, I *will* praise You at all times.

When my eyes are filled with tears, when my heart is ruptured and my head throbs from sorrow, my mouth will still, forever, continue to praise You.

PRAYER FOR TODAY

Lord, I *will* praise You at all times—even today, when I just don't feel like it. Because it really is true: You are always good.

Amen.

My comfort in my suffering is this: Your promise preserves my life.

PSALM 119:50 NIV

The LORD hears his people when they call to him for help. He rescues them from all their troubles.

PSALM 34:17–18 NLT

The LORD will continually guide you, and satisfy your desire in scorched places, and give strength to your bones; and you will be like a watered garden, and like a spring of water whose waters do not fail.

ISAIAH 58:11 NASB

> The LORD is close to the brokenhearted;
> he rescues those whose spirits are crushed.
> The righteous person faces many troubles,
> but the LORD comes to the rescue each time
>
> PSALM 34:18–19 NLT

YESTERDAY I FOUND MYSELF WEEPING AT THE SIGHT OF an elderly woman.

I sat on a bench overlooking the cliffs of Santa Cruz, California. A grandmotherly woman walked by. She looked to be in her seventies, wearing a drab tracksuit. She was still trim and active despite her craggy features and dowdy sense of style. She smiled away from me, looking toward her walking companion, and I was undone. I tried to hold back my tears until she passed, and then I just couldn't stop them.

Before she died, Amy wrote me a letter. In it she said, "I so wanted to grow old with you. . . . I didn't imagine cancer as a part of our lives—but I did imagine that we would be together no matter what. And so we are."

Except . . . now we are not.

Now it's just me growing old alone, wishing for, longing for, missing the little-old-lady version of Amy. The one in the frumpy tracksuit and comfortable sneakers, wearing an easy smile, joyful mischief in her emerald eyes, holding my hand tightly in her wrinkled fingers.

I miss my girl. Not just the woman I've loved all of my adult life, who thirty years ago honeymooned with me in this very spot. Not just the woman who, only eighteen months ago, sat on this bench next to me and leaned warmth into my side while we laughed beside the sea.

I miss the tender, loving old lady Amy would have become. I miss that happy, shiny old woman I know so well and love so deeply . . . but never got to meet.

Yesterday, when that gray-haired, smiling, rumpled grandmother ambled past me, I could see only the Amy that might have been, that version of my girl that never was. What else could I do but grieve my new poverty?

Ah, Jesus, be close to my broken heart now . . . . I need Your rescue . . . again.

PRAYER FOR TODAY

Christ Jesus, if You're close to the brokenhearted, then You must be near to me now. Help my spirit to recognize Yours today, so I can be rescued by Your love.

Amen.

O God, hear my cry for help. Pay attention to my prayer. From the remotest place on earth I call out to you in my despair. Lead me up to a rocky summit where I can be safe. Indeed, you are my shelter, a strong tower that protects me from the enemy.

PSALM 61:1–3 NET

"I will lead them. I will comfort those who mourn, bringing words of praise to their lips. May they have abundant peace, both near and far," says the LORD, who heals them.

ISAIAH 57:18–19 NLT

> The LORD helps the fallen and lifts those bent
> beneath their loads. . . . The LORD is close to
> all who call on him, yes, to all who call on
> him in truth.
>
> PSALM 145:14, 18 NLT

I WOKE UP THIS MORNING A LITTLE CONFUSED AND thought, "Hooray! Amy's coming home today!" I guess I was dreaming that Amy had gone away on a business trip or something.

Then I remembered.

Needless to say, today has been a l-o-n-g day. This relentless grief leaves me bent and doubled under its heavy load.

Help me, Jesus. Then help me some more. I'm calling on You now.
Amen.

PRAYER FOR TODAY

I'm calling on You, Lord! I don't know the right words to say, trapped here within this pain. So I'll just say what I do know: Jesus . . . Jesus . . . Jesus. Jesus . . . Jesus . . . Jesus . . .

Amen.

Though I walk in the midst of trouble, You will revive me; You will stretch forth Your hand against the wrath of my enemies, and Your right hand will save me.

PSALM 138:7 NASB

The salvation of the righteous comes from the LORD; he is their stronghold in time of trouble. The LORD helps them and delivers them.

PSALM 37:39–40 NIV

Fear not, for I am with you; be not dismayed, for I am your God; I will strengthen you, I will help you, I will uphold you with my righteous right hand.

ISAIAH 41:10 ESV

The LORD watches over the way of the righteous.

PSALM 1:6 NIV

Why am I so depressed? Why this turmoil within me? Put your hope in God, for I will still praise Him, my Savior and my God.

PSALM 43:5 HCSB

I FOUND THIS TODAY, LORD, AS I WAS WEEPING THROUGH one of Amy's journals.

She wrote this message to herself in January of 2015, about eight months before she discovered she had cancer. She had been reading Psalm 43 that week and left this note hidden in her writings. She never intended for anyone to see it but You and her.

ᔑ

Focus on hope. Let go of worry and anger.

I have seen God at work. I know God is powerful and nothing escapes his eye. Yet also see so much pain and downright mean people (who say they are Christians).

Focus on hope. Be anxious for nothing. Tell God.

My hope is in the Lord.

God—I am knocking on your door. Only you can deliver.

Discouragement and worry plague my mind. God—take them away! Do not let me be shaken. Do not let our family be shaken!

ॐ

Now that Amy is gone, I am struck by the way she lived out her own exhortation here, from health to weakness, from hope to fractured hope to unbreakable hope, from life to sorrow, through pain to death.

I think maybe today I will try to listen to her voice as she speaks Your words to my heart:

Put your hope in God, for I will still praise Him.

PRAYER FOR TODAY

God, I'm knocking on Your door. Only You can deliver me. I trust in You!

Amen.

Cast all your anxiety on him because he
cares for you.

1 PETER 5:7 NIV

I BOUGHT MYSELF A USED GUITAR TODAY. I'VE BEEN EYE-
ing it in the pawn shop window for a few weeks, and today I
decided I was feeling so anxious and just depressed enough
that a cheap guitar might help.

When Amy was pregnant with our son, many years
ago, we were young and poor. No TV, no movies, just the
two of us happy-ing our way through those heady days of
early life together. A worship-leader friend of mine had
given me a guitar, one of his spares, because I'd decided I
wanted to be the kind of father who could play a few songs
in the family room and get children singing, dancing, and
just enjoying time at home with mom and dad.

So just about every night, Amy and I would sit next
to each other on our reclaimed leather couch, she with a
book in hand, me with that Takamine guitar in my arms. I
spent nine months teaching myself how to play chords and
simple worship songs while she read and laughed at the

"Tarzan Baby" that danced to my stuttering music from within her bloated belly. And one of the songs I learned to play was scripture put to music, "I will cast all my cares upon you . . . ."

After Tony was born, one of the few things that would calm his colic was hearing me strum that guitar. (We soon learned that James Taylor was a better substitute for my amateurish work . . . and that's how JT became Amy's all-time favorite musician.) When Tony was a toddler, he used to sit on top of my guitar and bang on the strings because he enjoyed the sound.

As he grew, we did indeed hang out in our family room, playing, singing, and enjoying each other with my (still stuttering) guitar as the soundtrack for our lives. In junior high, he used my guitar to take lessons until he "graduated" to an electric version. When he finished college, I gave him that trusty old acoustic as a gift, a passing of the torch, so to speak.

In the spring of 2015 I began to have the yearning for a guitar in the house again, and I started saving my "allowance," planning to buy myself a new axe for my birthday in December. And then . . . well, you know what happened then. By December of 2015, suffice it to say that we had gone full circle and were now old and poor. No guitar for Mikey on that birthday.

About six or seven weeks before she died, I think in

late July or early August, Amy gave me a tin can with a bunch of twenty-dollar bills in it—her "allowance" money. She'd been saving it for months. She told me she wouldn't be needing it anymore and that when she was gone I should use it to buy "whatever you want." So today, when I was feeling anxious and troubled and heartbroken, I followed Amy's instructions and bought myself a used Yamaha guitar from a pawn shop window.

The way I figure it, my girl bought me this guitar today, a little leftover gift from the woman who gave me everything.

Now I think I'll go see if I remember the right chords for that scripture song of 1 Peter 5:7. I think strumming it will help to soothe me in times like this one, when I'm feeling so sad.

At least, I hope so. I really, really hope so.

PRAYER FOR TODAY

Jesus, thank You for being willing to take *all* the dirty, unpretty, distressing, and burdensome cares that I cast Your way today. I'm grateful You love me enough to do that.

Amen.

Then David continued, "Be strong and courageous, and do the work. Don't be afraid or discouraged, for the LORD God, my God, is with you. He will not fail you or forsake you."

1 CHRONICLES 28:20 NLT

AMY TOLD ME THIS STORY BACK IN 2013, AND I MADE HER write it down so I wouldn't forget it. Now that Amy is gone, I think I finally understand . . . .

༄

Last Monday my niece, Jane, and I were waiting for her ride, Amanda, to show up at a nearby park-and-ride lot. We were waiting just off the freeway, at the crossroads of a major highway. We parked near the entrance of the lot as we didn't know what kind of car Amanda would be driving.

While we were waiting, a shiny red car drove into the lot and parked in the empty space directly in front of us. We could see the face of the driver, a woman. She was just a few feet away, facing in our direction—but she didn't make eye contact with us. It was like she didn't even know we were there.

"That's not Amanda," I said to Jane, and so we kept chatting, but since this woman was directly in front of us, we could easily see everything she did.

She shut off the engine of her car, then immediately covered her face with both of her hands. She was sort of rubbing at her eyes with the palms of her hands. At first I thought maybe she was tired, but as we saw her there, it became clear she was crying. Not heaving sobs—more like tired and weary tears. She sat there in front of us weeping, wiping her eyes, resting her head on the steering wheel, and then finally gathering her composure. Before five minutes was over she started her car again and, without a glance at us, drove away.

Jane and I were silent for a moment, thinking.

"Do you think she just stopped here to cry?" I asked at last.

"I guess . . ." Jane answered.

Amanda showed up soon after. I hugged Jane goodbye and watched them drive away. But in my mind, this whole week since, I keep seeing that woman leaning into the steering wheel in her shiny red car. Weeping alone.

༄

PRAYER FOR TODAY

Lord God, my God, I'm awed that You're always with me. Because of You, I never have to weep alone. Thank You.

Amen.

The LORD is your keeper; the LORD is your shade on your right hand. The sun shall not strike you by day, nor the moon by night. The LORD will keep you from all evil; he will keep your life.

PSALM 121:5–7 ESV

For I have given rest to the weary and joy to the sorrowing.

JEREMIAH 31:25 NLT

God is our refuge and strength, a helper who is always found in times of trouble. Therefore we will not be afraid, though the earth trembles and the mountains topple into the depths of the seas, though its waters roar and foam and the mountains quake with its turmoil.

PSALM 46:1–3 HCSB

> But he said to me, "My grace is sufficient
> for you, for my power is made perfect in
> weakness." Therefore I will boast all the
> more gladly about my weaknesses, so that
> Christ's power may rest on me.
>
> 2 CORINTHIANS 12:9 NIV

I AM HAVING TROUBLE TODAY, READING THIS VERSE TO myself. Grace, for me? I do not feel it. Grace sufficient for my sorrow? I just can't see it. Christ's power made perfect in my weakness? I don't understand it, not yet at least. But I do hold something that gives me hope that someday I will understand how God's grace is at work during this moment in my life.

As she was dying, Amy's deepest sorrow was that she would miss her two grandchildren's special moments in life—birthdays, graduations, weddings. Neither of these children will have strong memories of their "Mimi." Amy knew that, and yet she *so* wanted them to know of her love. So in the weeks just before she died, Amy spent herself, all the energy she could muster, creating a priceless gift to leave behind. I hold it now, secured in a white box that's stickered with Amy's picture and labeled with her grand-children's names.

There are eighteen years' worth of memories here, hand-written personal notes, an occasional picture to make a child smile, and maybe a rare sentimental token (or two), all lifted from Amy's life gone by. They're kept safe inside birthday cards, graduation cards, and even wedding cards, prepared lovingly for each of her grandchildren—from the Mimi they barely got to know.

Tomorrow I will give the first card—Amy's first love note—to her oldest grandchild.

I don't think four-year-old Genevieve will really understand what her Mimi has done for her on her birth-day, the unfathomable grace that's been bestowed on her, not yet at least. But someday this little girl will find she has amassed a collection of tender, happy, precious, priceless moments that always appeared on her special days, every envelope festooned with Amy's smiling, shining face, and written—each and every card—by a dying hand moved by love that refused to end.

One day our little Genevieve will grow up. Will marry. Will become a mother herself . . . and then, I think, yes, maybe then she'll understand.

One day soon, I hope, I too will grow up. Will move past

this constant grief. Will read 2 Corinthians 2:9 again . . . and, yes, I hope maybe then I too will understand.

PRAYER FOR TODAY

Jesus, today help me discover firsthand what it means for Your grace to be sufficient for me.

Amen.

He has said, I will never leave you or abandon
you. This is why we can confidently say,

The Lord is my helper
and I won't be afraid.
What can people do to me?
HEBREWS 13:5–6 CEB

SCREAMING

Maybe I'm getting worse. Hard to know. On Thursday I'll go for an appointment and they'll tell me. Already expecting bad news. But . . . I still believe in miracles.

—AMY NAPPA

JOURNAL ENTRY, JULY 8, 2016

> For His anger is but for a moment, His favor
> is for life; weeping may endure for a night,
> but joy comes in the morning.
>
> PSALM 30:5 NKJV

TWO RANDOM THOUGHTS TODAY:

1. I've been going to a grief support group lately. Yesterday when I sat in the group, I thought, *Wow, there are so many broken people here, with truly devastating stories to tell. Somebody needs to do something to help these people.* Today I'm wondering if I might need to be "somebody" (though I have no idea what that would mean, Lord). Something for me to think about.

2. A woman at the grief group yesterday told me, "Amy wouldn't want you to be sad, so put a smile on your face and be happy." I almost laughed at her ignorance. Does she think my grief is a choice I've made? That I want to feel this brokenhearted and paralyzed every day? That's kind of like telling a crippled man, "Amy wouldn't want you

to have a broken spine, so stop having a broken spine."

At this point, the hard truth is that I can't choose my feelings, despite my best efforts. I just wake up every morning feeling lonely and sad, and then later, after the day has blurred by, I go to bed at night feeling even more lonely and sad. Joy used to be such an ordinary thing for me, and now sadness is my new normal.

Apparently I am failing at grief.

I don't know what to do about that. Yet I'm still here, waking up each new morning, so I guess that means You are doing something in me even though I don't know what it is yet. As the Scripture says, "Weeping may endure for a night, but joy comes in the morning."

Amen.

Bring the morning to me, Jesus . . . Jesus . . . Jesus . . . bring the morning.

PRAYER FOR TODAY

Lord, here's something: Morning came again today. I think that means Your joy is headed my way, right? (I'm definitely looking forward to that.)

Amen.

I say to the LORD, "You are my Lord; apart
from you I have no good thing."

PSALM 16:2 NIV

IT'S LATE AT NIGHT, AND I CAN'T SLEEP. FOR SOME REASON
lately, my body can't relax until after 1:28 in the morning. I
keep telling myself that I don't need to mark that moment,
that waiting and watching the clock tick over to 1:29 A.M.
isn't a productive thing in my life, but my brain refuses to
listen.

So this may just be the sleep deprivation talking, but
I've been thinking about some things a lot tonight, and I
might as well write them down here . . . .

My girl had a fondness for men with Middle Eastern
features (lucky me).

She also liked musicians.

And she *loved* the Psalms.

This makes me wonder . . .

*How you gettin' on with King David, honey? (Tell him I
said "hey," and thanks for Psalm 16.)*

PRAYER FOR TODAY

God, apart from You I have no good thing—so it's a really good thing that I have You. Thank You so much.

Amen.

> For God has not given us a spirit of fear, but
> of power and of love and of a sound mind.
>
> 2 TIMOTHY 1:7 NKJV

AMY WAS *NOT* A LARGE PERSON.

If she stretched, she barely scraped 5'3" on a measuring tape. When we got engaged she weighed a whopping 115 pounds. Thirty years later, she weighed a steady 118. Her dress size was 4, shirt size always a "small." "Petite" was a word often used to describe my girl. She was beautiful, yes—stunning, actually—but never an imposing figure.

So why is it that having that tiny little woman next to me always made me feel so safe?

Why does her absence stir within me such irrational fear?

Today I sat in church, eyes closed, stomach fluttering. I was surrounded by familiar faces, many of whom had hugged and cooked and prayed and cried alongside us while Amy fought her way through cancer's hard way home. I know these people, and they know me. Yet without

Amy sitting in her normal seat beside me, I felt exposed, unwelcome.

Afraid.

It made no sense. The most frightening thing about my church is that sometimes the drummer gets "happy" and bangs those tin cans a little louder than expected. But logic was a feckless thing for me this morning.

My doctors tell me that irrational anxiety is a normal side effect of grief response and severe depression, so I guess I must learn to live with this frequent, baseless, heart-pounding fear. But I don't like it.

So today, still trembling inside myself after the service, I ducked my head and prepared to make a stealth run to the exit when one of Amy's friends stopped me. (What's her name again? I can't remember. Amy kept track of names for me . . .)

"Mike," she said, "I don't know if this will mean anything to you or not, but while we were singing I suddenly felt very strongly that God wanted me to share a scripture with you."

"OK," I said. I waited.

And then she said, "God has not given us a spirit of fear, but of power and of love and of a sound mind. Does that mean anything to you?"

I couldn't answer. I was too busy crying.

Thank You, Jesus, for remembering me when I was

afraid today. For giving me power, love, and a sound mind, even when I still feel afraid.

For I, the LORD your God, hold your right hand;
it is I who say to you, "Fear not, I am the one
who helps you."

ISAIAH 41:13 ESV

Whenever I am afraid, I will trust in You. In God (I will praise His word), in God I have put my trust; I will not fear. What can flesh do to me?

PSALM 56:3-4 NKJV

Jesus said, "Don't let your hearts be troubled. Trust in God, and trust in me."

JOHN 14:1 NCV

> Those who sow in tears shall reap in joy. He who continually goes forth weeping, bearing seed for sowing, shall doubtless come again with rejoicing.
>
> PSALM 126:5–6 NKJV

HERE'S WHAT THEY DON'T TEACH YOU IN PREMARITAL counseling or couples' Sunday school classes:

The best parts of marriage aren't the big moments— not the wedding anniversaries or Valentine's Days or Disney family vacations. The real treasures of matrimony are the small moments, the indistinguishable, easily neglected ones where you're just two people breathing comfortably in a room together.

Holding hands while you watch TV.

Reading books beside each other in bed.

Recounting the boring details of your day while you make dinner.

Jumping off the couch to get her Chapstick because she might kiss you lightly on the lips before she slathers it on.

Deciding that, yes, both of you do like Meghan Trainor's music after all.

Laughing at the dog because he's scared of your dancing when Meghan Trainor's music is on.

Hearing "I love you" mumbled in your ear every night just before you drift off to sleep—and again after the alarm wakes you both up in the morning.

These are the moments you long for when they're gone. You miss having someone to "do nothing" with, someone who'll happily share the unexciting episodes of your everyday existence just because they like being near you as much as you like being near them.

It's in these times I miss Amy most. Times like right now.

Sheesh, will I ever stop crying?

PRAYER FOR TODAY

Lord, we have sown many tears, You and I, mourning the countless little losses taken away by death. How about if we begin reaping in joy, even just a little bit, today?

Amen.

LORD, don't hold back your tender mercies from me. Let your unfailing love and faithfulness always protect me. For troubles surround me—too many to count! My sins pile up so high I can't see my way out. They outnumber the hairs on my head. I have lost all courage. Please, LORD, rescue me! Come quickly, LORD, and help me.

PSALM 40:11–13 NLT

The LORD pays attention to the godly and hears their cry for help.

PSALM 34:15 NET

He will shelter you with his wings; you will find safety under his wings. His faithfulness is like a shield or a protective wall. You need not fear the terrors of the night.

PSALM 91:4–5 NET

> Now when Mary came to where Jesus was
> and saw him, she fell at his feet, saying to
> him, "Lord, if you had been here, my brother
> would not have died." When Jesus saw her
> weeping, and the Jews who had come with
> her also weeping, he was deeply moved in
> his spirit and . . . . Jesus wept. So the Jews
> said, "See how he loved him!" But some of
> them said, "Could not he who opened the
> eyes of the blind man also have kept this
> man from dying?"
>
> JOHN 11:32–33, 35–37 ESV

IT IS THE FRIDAY AFTER THANKSGIVING. BLACK FRIDAY AS they call it in retail. Though I'm supposed to be preparing to celebrate the birth of Christ, I find myself instead thinking about Mary, the sister of Lazarus, and how she wept with Christ.

Late last night, when I couldn't sleep, I too fell facedown at Jesus' feet, nose buried in the musty carpet of my bedroom, asking a question similar to hers:

"Lord, where were You? If You'd been paying attention, my wife would not have died."

And like the Jews, I'm asking myself today, "Couldn't He who opened the eyes of the blind man . . . who raised Lazarus from the dead . . . couldn't He have kept Amy from dying?"

One year ago today, Amy and I set up our Christmas tree in the family room of our house. When I say that, what I really mean is that Amy set it up and I watched.

It was always our tradition to decorate the tree the day after Thanksgiving. This was probably our second-favorite night of the year—second only to Christmas itself. Amy's job was to assemble the artificial tree, to lovingly unpack all the ornaments, and to make beauty out of the ragtag decorations we'd collected over our last few decades together.

My job was to make sure we had plenty of Christmas music. Originally working with piles of CDs, I finally got smart and put all our holiday music onto a few playlists. So after getting the Christmas supplies out of storage, my job was really just to enjoy watching my girl do her thing with them. It was a treasure to watch her work. She was rarely more beautiful than when her heart was fixed on Christmas.

On this After-Thanksgiving-Day last year, Amy was still struggling through difficult chemotherapy treatments. She was unable to eat solid food, barely 100 pounds, and surviving solely on fourteen-hour-a-day infusions of IV nutrition. And yet she was so filled with joy.

She laughed and sang along to Christmas songs, and she delighted in pulling her ornaments out of storage. In our house, there are no cookie-cutter decorations. Every ornament for our tree has a history, comes with a story. "Tony made this lambkin ornament in grade school." "You gave me this Mickey ornament for my birthday." "I've had this elf since I was a child—it was my mom's. I have to find a good place to hide it in the tree so Tony can find it next time he comes over."

When our tree was finally ready, we indulged in our family's second Christmas tradition.

Amy made two mugs of hot cocoa, gave one to me and kept the other for herself. We turned off all the lights except those on the Christmas tree. We sat close to each other on the couch, held hands, and sipped from our steaming cups as we watched the tree lights wink and grin in the darkened family room.

My girl was so happy she started sobbing next to me. "I love Christmas," she said to me, gripping my hand in tight little squeezes, making the couch tremble as she let her tears flow. "I'm so glad I'm here for it."

"Me too," I said. Me too.

The tree lights flickered and danced. We let silence be our conversation for a bit, while Kenny Loggins serenaded us with "Walking in the Air" (Amy's favorite Christmas song). We didn't say it out loud, but I think we both knew then that maybe . . . probably . . . it was going to be our last Christmas together on this earth.

Now it's a year later. Only one year. Such a short time, really, even though it feels like ages have gone by. I'm staring at the space where our giant tree is supposed to go.

And wondering what I'm supposed to do now.

PRAYER FOR TODAY

I feel lost today, Jesus. Alone. When I weep, will You share my sorrow and weep alongside me? For some reason, I think that'll make me feel better. I love You.

Amen.

> No eye has seen, no ear has heard, and no
> mind has imagined what God has prepared
> for those who love him.
>
> 1 CORINTHIANS 2:9 NLT

LATELY I FIND MYSELF THINKING "AMY WOULD'VE" AND "Amy used to" a lot.

I mean, *a lot.*

For instance, tonight I stood in the street in the freezing cold, watching our preschool-aged granddaughter perform a sweet little ballet at a local tree-lighting event downtown. *Amy would've just loved this,* I thought almost instantly. *She would've cheered and teared up and been full of joy.* I looked over at Amy's sister Jody, who was standing next to me, also weeping, and knew I wasn't the only one thinking those thoughts.

Every year, Amy and I had a tradition of watching our favorite holiday movies in the days between Thanksgiving and Christmas. Today I saw *Love Actually* in a stack of DVDs and thought, *Amy used to love watching this movie. It made her cry every time.*

Once, some years ago, she was having a really bad day.

I hurriedly took a cue from one of the characters in the movie and scribbled a little sign for her.

"To me, you are perfect," it said.

I stood in a doorway and held it up to my chest for her the next time she walked by. She burst into tears and hugged me for a long time. Then she felt better, and I forgot all about it.

After she died, I found that scrap-paper sign in a keepsake box of hers. She'd saved it, treasured it, for years, and I never knew. Amy used to do stuff like that, secretly save silly, sentimental mementos I made for her.

Amy would've . . .

Amy used to . . .

As soon as these thoughts appear in my brain, they're almost always followed by *I would've* . . . and *I used to* . . . As in, *I would've loved this with Amy* . . . and *I used to love being that with Amy* . . .

My girl is dead and gone. I know this. She is safe, happy, free. But I am none of those things. So I sit here suffering, thinking, *I would've loved to watch tonight's preschool ballet with Amy at my side.* And I used to love watching *Love Actually* with her and holding her hand when it was time for her to cry. No more. I find this unbelievably hard.

Still . . .

In the weeks before she died, I handwrote one last note for my girl:

"No eye has seen, no ear has heard, and no mind has imagined what God has prepared for those who love him (1 Corinthians 2:9)."

I used a black, fine-point Sharpie on a pink index card. I hung it at her eye level, on the table next to her hospice bed, so she would see it whenever she woke up. It was a promise, I thought, of what she would soon find in heaven. I still believe that.

But lately I've also been wondering: What if this promise is meant for me too?

Amy is experiencing 1 Corinthians 2:9 fully in the presence of joy. But what if God intends for me to experience it too, at least in part, here on earth? What unimaginable wonders has God prepared for me before I join her?

I don't know, but I do know that . . .

Amy would've loved that.

Be my rock of refuge, to which I can always go; give the command to save me, for you are my rock and my fortress.

PSALM 71:3 NIV

Come to Me, all you who labor and are heavy laden, and I will give you rest. Take My yoke upon you and learn from Me, for I am gentle and lowly in heart, and you will find rest for your souls.

MATTHEW 11:28–29 NKJV

> Heal me, O LORD, and I shall be healed;
> save me, and I shall be saved, for you are
> my praise.
>
> JEREMIAH 17:14 ESV

ONE YEAR AGO TODAY ON DECEMBER 8, 2015, I WAS kidnapped—I mean "escorted"—to the hospital by my friend Jimmy. Apparently I was having a medical emergency brought on by previously undiagnosed Crohn's disease. Go figure. Emergency surgery was scheduled for early the next morning.

Lying in an uncomfortable hospital bed late that night, I texted Amy. I told her (just in case I didn't make it through) that I loved her more than any earthly thing. She told me to stop it because I was making her cry, and that she loved me so, so much. She was in the middle of chemotherapy, and she was scared for me.

Coming out of surgery the next morning, apparently I quit breathing (twice), and they resuscitated me both times. Sometimes I wish they hadn't done that. It would've saved me a lot of physical pain and emotional suffering. But I also realize that if I had died that day, the next nine months would have been unforgivably awful for Amy. So I guess God knew what He was doing.

Amy wasn't able to visit me in the hospital because of immune deficiencies she was experiencing from chemotherapy. I was terribly alone (a foretaste of what was to come, I suppose). The nurses kept finding me sobbing in the dark, in my hospital bed, saying, "I miss my wife. I just miss my wife." I spent my birthday just trying to breathe and not throw up. A few days later, as a surprise for me, Amy's dad brought my girl to the sidewalk outside my hospital room. She called me on my cell phone. I dragged myself to the window to talk to her, and I cried at the beautiful sight of her ninety-eight-pound body and the sound of her happy voice in my ear.

She wept with worry over me and with joy at being able to see me in the window. To show me she was feeling better and that I shouldn't worry about her, Amy danced a cute little Irish jig on the sidewalk.

I can still see her puppet-like bouncing, big grin on her face, dancing just for me out there in the freezing Colorado winter. That memory makes me smile.

She told me she loved me so much and couldn't wait for me to come home. When I finally got home, she was waiting for me, arms open wide, wearing the "hugging shirt"—a shirt we kept sterilized at all times so she could hug and be hugged without risking infection. I still have that hugging shirt, you know.

It's a red-and-white, button-up, western-style dress shirt with her all-time favorite, Mickey Mouse, on it. Amy bought it for me five years ago, during our twenty-fifth wedding anniversary trip to Walt Disney World. I used to wear that shirt a lot; it made me smile and feel warm inside. I saw it in my closet today and realized I haven't worn that Mickey Mouse shirt since September.

Today I am all healed up from that kidnapping—I mean, from being escorted into emergency surgery. Now, though, it is my heart that is deathly ill. There is no surgery for the soul, and no beautiful, ninety-eight-pound girl to dance like a marionette and make me smile in my pain.

But I am not alone.

The Great Physician stands nearby, so I will ask of Him the same that Jeremiah did a few thousand years ago: Heal me, O Lord, and I shall be healed. Save me, Jesus, and I shall be saved, for You are my praise.

PRAYER FOR TODAY

Lord Jesus, if You heal me, I *will* be healed. If You save me from this sorrow, then I *will* be saved. So . . . heal me, Jesus. Save me, for You are my praise.

Amen.

> Do not be eager in your heart to be angry,
> for anger resides in the bosom of fools.
>
> ECCLESIASTES 7:9 NASB

TODAY I FIND MYSELF FEELING ANGRY THAT, FOR SO many years, I had a genuinely happy marriage.

There's snow on the ground outside, but the air is warm and sunshiny. Christmas praises ring through my stereo, often sung by people who have no idea what they're really proclaiming to the world. A stack of presents is waiting to be wrapped, piled carefully, and tagged in my family room. A similar stack of interesting books sits waiting to be read, and a backlog of my favorite Christmas movies is demanding to be watched this year.

In other words, today is a perfect day . . . except that I remember too well what these kinds of days were like when Amy inhabited them with me.

I remember the comfort of her nearness, the joy of hearing her voice singing along to the stereo. I remember my home smelling like cinnamon coffee cake on cold winter mornings, the happiness in her eyes as she carefully folded and taped every single package for our nieces and grand-daughter. I remember her insistence that I shake my presents, knowing I'd never really guess what they were because she'd sneaked in a few rattling things among the Captain America toys and Mickey Mouse T-shirts, just to throw me off. In my mind, I can even smell the remnants of her shampoo from when I'd lean over to kiss her neck and tell her how beautiful she was while making Christmas cookies just for me. (She always thought I was joking, but I was serious about that!)

And I find myself complaining to the walls, "If I'd had a rotten marriage, if Amy had been a bitter, unhappy shrew, maybe I'd be happier today. Maybe I'd even be almost relieved to have a little peace and solitude."

But that's not the way it was, nor the way it is.

So today instead of peace and solitude, I find myself feeling isolated, lonely, angry—mourning and weeping over golden days gone by.

"Was it worth it?", I grumble. This grief is such a costly thing.

"Do not be eager in your heart to be angry," the preacher of Ecclesiastes says softly to me, "for anger resides in the bosom of fools."

Sigh. He is right.

So was it worth it? Is this pain I suffer today (and tomorrow and the next) a fair price to pay for so many happy days with Amy in my past?

Yes. A hundred times over, yes.

A thousand days like today would be a bargain to pay for just one of those snowy Christmas Saturdays with Amy. So, even though I suffer what those happy days past are costing me now, I have to admit I'm more grateful than even I can understand to have known them, to have taken their familiar joy for granted.

I have known great love, and great things always come with a steep price.

Today's sorrow, I think, is not too high a price to pay.

PRAYER FOR TODAY

When I'm tempted to anger and depression today, Father, remind me that I still don't know the end of my story—and that I can trust You instead.

Amen.

Be careful what you think, because your
thoughts run your life.
PROVERBS 4:23 NCV

For we do not have a high priest who cannot sympathize with our weaknesses, but One who has been tempted in all things as we are, yet without sin. Therefore let us draw near with confidence to the throne of grace, so that we may receive mercy and find grace to help in time of need.

In peace I will lie down and sleep, for you alone, LORD, make me dwell in safety.

PSALM 4:8 NIV

For You have delivered my soul from death.
Have You not kept my feet from falling, that I
may walk before God in the light of the living?

PSALM 56:13 NKJV

Whom have I in heaven but you? I desire
you more than anything on earth. My health
may fail, and my spirit may grow weak, but
God remains the strength of my heart; he is
mine forever.

PSALM 73:25–26 NLT

AMY AND I TOOK A PICTURE OF OURSELVES ON CHRIST-
mas Day 2015. We're standing in front of our tree, and just
above our heads in the background you can see a Pixar ball
ornament that she gave me as a special present. I had hung
it at the top of the tree only moments before.

I am standing behind my girl in the picture, arms
wrapped around her. She's smiling at the camera, clinging
tightly to my left arm with both of her hands. We're both
wearing handmade knit caps, she because she was bald from
chemotherapy, me because I was weak and freezing and still
trying to recover from emergency surgery two weeks before.

I look like hell in the picture: thin, face gaunt, eyes
dull, smile forced, my shoulder so emaciated it almost looks
like my left sleeve is empty.

Amy, on the other hand, is beautiful.

There is honest joy in her eyes, her weight is back up over one hundred pounds, life is blushing in her cheeks, and hope is lighting up her face. Circumstance-wise, it was easily our worst Christmas ever, yet she was so grateful. She loved having that moment with me and with her family. She radiated warmth and sunshine and happiness all day long—all season long. She was the embodiment of Psalm 73:26. There she stood, health failing, spirit growing weaker, and yet God was indeed the strength of her heart.

Just being with Amy that last Christmas, even in all my physical pain and emotional sorrow, was truly a gift from God. She was joy incarnate that day . . . that last time in my life when December 25 would be a pure, happy day.

Tomorrow is Christmas, the start of a new kind of Christmas for me.

Will God be the strength of my heart this year, be mine forever, just as He was for Amy last holiday season?

PRAYER FOR TODAY

My health seems like it's failing. My body feels weak (and my soul too). But You, Jesus, are *mine* forever. Help me find strength in that truth today.

Amen.

But You, O LORD, are a shield about me, my glory, and the One who lifts my head.

PSALM 3:3 NASB

The LORD gives strength to his people; the LORD blesses his people with peace.

PSALM 29:11 NCV

I will be with you always, even until the end of this age.

MATTHEW 28:20 NCV

Yet I call this to mind, and therefore I have
hope: Because of the LORD's faithful love we
do not perish, for His mercies never end.
They are new every morning; great is Your
faithfulness! I say: The LORD is my portion,
therefore I will put my hope in Him.

LAMENTATIONS 3:21–24 HCSB

IT IS ALMOST THE NEW YEAR, AND HERE'S HOW THE INNER
dialogue in my head sounds today:

OPTIMIST: OK, Mikey. Just a few more days, then you
can leave 2016 behind; 2017 will be a fresh
start.

PESSIMIST: What good is a fresh start if Amy's not
there to share it?

OPTIMIST: It's the last gift she left behind for you.
Fresh start. New beginning. New hope.
New life.

PESSIMIST: But how can any new start really be fresh,
when all I really want is the old life, the

one that ended with Amy and me being old folks together thirty years from now? *That* was fresh and exciting and happy.

OPTIMIST: I know, of course, that would've been great. But that's not an option. So take what she left you, and make something new and beautiful out of it.

PESSIMIST: Now you're just talking out of your hairy posterior.

OPTIMIST: Leave my hairy behind out of this. Think about how awful 2016 was. Aren't you glad to leave that behind?

PESSIMIST: It was more than awful. It was like dying without ever getting the relief of being dead.

OPTIMIST: Right. See? 2017! New beginning! Fresh start!

PESSIMIST: But Amy was in 2016. That makes it precious. That makes it irreplaceable.

OPTIMIST: Well, but . . .

PESSIMIST: When I step from 2016 into 2017, Amy is completely gone from my life. There will never be another year with her in it.

OPTIMIST: Yeah, OK, but . . .

PESSIMIST: I will never be truly happy again. And neither will you.

OPTIMIST: Um . . .

PESSIMIST: You stink at cheering me up.

OPTIMIST: All right. Here's the way it is. Amy is gone. I can't cheer you up about that, so I'm not going to try. But you can't just keep sobbing in the aisles at Walmart. You're scaring the workers.

PESSIMIST: I know.

OPTIMIST: Your wife loved you more than anything this side of heaven. She told you to find a way to be happy without her. So what are you going to do with that in 2017?

PESSIMIST: I don't know. She didn't know what she was asking of me. She asked too much.

OPTIMIST: Here's a hint. What song did she pick to have sung at your wedding?

PESSIMIST: "Great Is Thy Faithfulness." From Lamentations 3.

OPTIMIST: She loved that song and that scripture. "His mercies never end. They are new every morning. . . . The Lord is my portion, therefore I will put my hope in Him." She believed that. She lived it, and she died that way too.

PESSIMIST: Mm.

OPTIMIST: And here's another hint: one of Amy's

favorite movies was *The Shawshank Redemption*.

PESSIMIST: Sigh. "Get busy living, or get busy dying." Andy Dufresne.

OPTIMIST: And?

PESSIMIST: "Remember Red, hope is a good thing, maybe the best of things, and no good thing ever dies."

OPTIMIST: Right. So?

PESSIMIST: Pfft. *Hope* is just another meaningless word. I don't want hope or a fresh start. I want Amy. That's all I want.

OPTIMIST: I wish you could have her, but you can't.

[Long pause]

OPTIMIST: So what are you going to do for the one thing Amy loved more than anything this side of heaven?

[Longer pause]

PESSIMIST: You're mean, and you smell funny too.

OPTIMIST: I know. Deal with it. Like it or not, Amy entrusted her most precious possession to you (and Jesus, of course). So what are you going to do with *you*, Mikey? What will you choose?

PESSIMIST: Sigh.

[Long silence]

PESSIMIST: Hope, I guess. Fresh start. Ready or not, here I come. Woohoo. Sigh.

OPTIMIST: Right. And maybe you can finally cut your hair and start shaving again, and—

PESSIMIST: Whoa, bro. One baby step at a time. One at a time. Now go find me a new box of tissues because I've used this one up already . . .

PRAYER FOR TODAY

Lord Jesus, I choose hope. Help me choose hope! You, Lord, are my hope.

Amen.

HOPING

I hope that when I'm gone you'll still see God's goodness. Still see His love for you. Still find joy in each day.

—AMY NAPPA

JOURNAL ENTRY, JULY 8, 2016

I would have despaired unless I had believed that I would see the goodness of the LORD in the land of the living. Wait for the LORD; be strong and let your heart take courage; yes, wait for the LORD.

PSALM 27:13–14 NASB

A MESSAGE TO MY FRIENDS:

Hello, Loved Ones.

Here's my Top Five for today:

1. I've been applying for jobs and even had one interview this month. Everything was going well until they asked why I was interested in making a change. I had practiced answering that question because I knew it was coming. I intended to say, "I'm looking to make a fresh start after losing my wife to cancer." Instead, I started crying uncontrollably, right in the middle of the conference room. I didn't get the job.

2. I dream of Amy every night, have dreamed of her every single night for the past 135 days. I used to wake up crying afterward, but now I actually look forward to seeing her in my sleep. It's the only time I feel just a little bit of peace. I think that when I have that first night when I don't dream of her, it will probably mean I am finally starting to heal. I'd like that. But until then, I'll just keep looking for her in my dreams.

3. Yes, I've tried going back to write that novel I started when Amy was alive. She begged me to complete it before she died, but I just couldn't do it. And no, I haven't been able to even open that folder on my computer since she passed away. It just seems pointless to write a story she'll never read. I'm thankful that my publisher is very patient. They tell me that they think I'll feel differently in the future and that I am worth the wait. Yes, they are kinder than necessary.

4. Despite my obvious, constant depression, I do want you to know that I am trying to move forward. I know that, were Amy here, she'd be running out of patience with me and my fixation on grief. So I'm trying. It's just hard without her to help me. I got so used to depending on her wisdom ("Honey, what do

you think about . . ."), relying on her strength and her unwavering loyalty, and resting in her tender ability to repair me whenever I was broken. So now I feel stuck in this moment, forced to wait until God Himself leads me out of it. It is necessary, but it's also a relentless, desolate way to live. Feel free to pray about that.

5. Now that the calendar has changed over, it is the true beginning of my "After Amy" years. I will move forward, and maybe I'll throw out a few surprises for you as this year moves on. But for now, I'm still just a broken, lonely thing trying to heal, trying to follow King David's advice in Psalm 27:14, "Wait for the LORD; be strong and let your heart take courage; yes, wait for the LORD."

6. I'll let you know how it goes.

PRAYER FOR TODAY

Ah Lord, I would despair if not for You. I believe it's true that I'll see Your goodness here in the land of the living. Open my eyes so I can see. Thank You, Jesus.

Amen.

> But God knows the way that I take, and when
> he has tested me, I will come out like gold.
>
> JOB 23:10 NCV

BEFORE SHE DIED, I ASKED AMY TO WRITE HER OWN OBIT-uary. I just couldn't do it. I told her I would put in the appropriate dates, but she had to do the rest. So she did.

This is how she wanted to be remembered . . .

ༀ

Amy Wakefield Nappa was born on November 10, 1963, in Portsmouth, VA, to Norm and Winnie Wakefield. She moved to heaven on Sunday, September 11, 2016.

Amy was a sister, a wife, a mother, a grandmother, and a friend. She loved her family and her friends dearly. Her greatest joys were to spend time with family, to hang out with her friends, to laugh, and to mentor those a little behind her in the journey of life.

Amy loved Jesus with all her heart, and her greatest desire was to be remembered as a woman who shined the love of Jesus.

༄

Looking at this now, months later, I feel a touch of pride. She was everything she said in this obituary—and much more. She left out the parts about how she was a successful business executive, a bestselling and award-winning author, a woman whose published works influenced the lives of millions of people in nations all over the planet, a speaker to thousands, and (because she ranked it highly in her life) an annual volunteer at the "Imagination Station" of our local VBS productions.

Amy changed the world. I've asked myself how she did it, how one little woman living an obscure life in a small town in Colorado could make such a difference for millions of people. The only answer I can come up with is this:

Amy's greatest desire really was to be remembered as a woman who shined the love of Jesus.

That was just who she was; it was natural for her. And God used Amy just being herself to shine His love through her and spray it out into the world. And when she suffered, when her body failed her and her faith was tested in the extreme, she was still just Amy being Amy, shining His love on all of us who were near.

It was the worst time of my life.

And the most extraordinary time I've known.

God knew the way that Amy took, and like Job of old, at the final end she came out shining . . . like gold.

PRAYER FOR TODAY

Dear Father, I think I'd like to shine—just a little bit. When I'm tested today, may Your Spirit be the help I need to come out of everything shining. Like gold.

Amen.

The LORD will be your everlasting light, and
your days of sorrow will end.

ISAIAH 60:20 NIV

I'VE DISCOVERED THAT THE THINGS YOU REALLY MISS
when you lose a loved one are the not-so-obvious ones.

I mean, of course you miss the obvious things—her
touch, her laugh, seeing her smile when you walk into the
room, the warmth of her frame pressed into yours, holding
her hand, the scent of her life filling your home, the gentle
weight of her body sleeping quietly beside you. But you also
miss the unexpected things:

The joy of anticipating her arrival home.

The way her spirit filled your house when she was in it.

The comfort of feeling obligated to someone because
you just longed for nothing more than to be obligated
to her.

Those little, loving obligations are what I'm missing
most right now. I find when I go somewhere, I want to text
and tell her I made it there safely. But there's no one who
cares that I made it to Walmart today. When it's almost

time for dinner, I want to ask her, "What do you want to eat tonight?" But of course, no one cares whether I order Chinese takeout or have cold cereal for dinner.

I want to tell her, "Hey, I made your Academy Awards ballot today!" and, "Let's take Friday off work and go see that movie you wanted to see" and, "I put gas in your car so you should be fine going to the airport and back on Thursday." And I'm realizing that the reason I struggle to write now is because, despite what I pretended, I always wrote for her.

Every book, every article, it always mattered to me because it mattered to her, because she wanted me to do it, because she thought my writing was worth reading. I have no one like that in my life now, no one who makes me want to work so, so hard to delight them with silly words strung in rows on a page.

This is what I miss right now, the salvation of all those little obligations, the unfiltered joy I felt from just being able to make her happy. That, I've learned, is what made me happy, what gave me purpose.

It is tempting to think I will always mourn these little losses, to assume my best days are behind me and that only sorrow awaits in my tomorrows. I have believed that from time to time these past lonely months.

But today I saw Isaiah 60:20. It felt as if I were reading it for the first time:

The Lord will be your everlasting light, and your days of sorrow will end.

Did God really say that? Can it be true for a broken thing like me?

It has been hard for me to have any real hope for my future since my wife died. This morning, though, I read a promise of Scripture and almost believed it for myself. That feels new. Those words from Isaiah have given me something today that seems different than yesterday:

I have hope that someday I'll have hope again.

Hey, it's a start, right?

PRAYER FOR TODAY

God, You promised that days of sorrow would end. I know that takes time, but how about if You and I work toward that a little more today?

Amen.

It is good to wait quietly for deliverance from the LORD.

LAMENTATIONS 3:26 HCSB

I waited patiently for the LORD to help me, and he turned to me and heard my cry. He lifted me out of the pit of despair, out of the mud and the mire. He set my feet on solid ground and steadied me as I walked along.

PSALM 40:1–2 NLT

We are hard-pressed on every side, yet not crushed; we are perplexed, but not in despair; persecuted, but not forsaken; struck down, but not destroyed.

2 CORINTHIANS 4:8–9 NKJV

Because you are my help, I sing in the shadow of your wings. I cling to you; your right hand upholds me.

PSALM 63:7–8 NIV

> Let me hear of your unfailing love each morning, for I am trusting you. Show me where to walk, for I give myself to you.
>
> PSALM 143:8 NLT

A MESSAGE TO MY FRIENDS:

Hello,

Several of you have reached out to check in on me recently, mentioned that you are worried about me—which is so kind. I know I've not posted much of significance lately. Sorry. Every time I sit down to update, it becomes just another psalm of pain and despair, and you've already endured too much of that over this past year. You deserve better.

Suffice it to say that I miss my girl.

I feel her absence as keenly right now as I did in the moment when I put my ear to her chest and found her spirit had already gone. I dream of her every night. I wake with tears every morning.

I miss her.

So I've decided no longer to simply wait for hope, to pray for hope, but to begin looking for hope. She gave me Psalm 143:8 as a gift in her journal, so this is now my theme for each day. *I am trusting you, God. Show me how to walk in hope.*

Thank you, my friends, for loving me, and for worrying about me, just a little.

PRAYER FOR TODAY

Jesus, let me hear of Your unfailing love this morning, for I am trusting You.

Amen.

Now let your unfailing love comfort me, just
as you promised me, your servant. Surround
me with your tender mercies so I may live,
for your instructions are my delight.

PSALM 119:76–77 NLT

IT SURPRISES ME SOMETIMES HOW GOD CHOOSES TO
sprinkle little comforts into my soul. This morning it happened with an unexpected memory:

One year ago today I woke up to the sound of Amy
laughing.

It was her birthday, and she'd unhooked her IV nutrition and wandered into the living room to wait for me
to wake up. She was still kind of beat up from her latest
chemotherapy, but she decided to check Facebook while
she waited. She saw a post of mine from late the night
before, addressed to a group of our friends who followed
her medical progress. It went like this . . .

All right friends, here's the official story:

*"Gosh, Mike is so sweet—did you see that he shaved (most
of?) his head in support of his poor, cancer-stricken wife?"*

Got that memorized? Good.

Now, here's what really happened . . .

Amy has cut my hair ever since we were engaged, meaning I haven't paid for a haircut in twenty-nine years. Why start now? That's like twelve whole bucks better spent on comics. So my girl tells me this week it's time to get a haircut. "Sure," I say, "no problem." And tonight, after she goes to bed, I pull out the electric clippers.

How hard can it be? See, it's easy as . . . oops. Well, I can fix th— Wait a minute. Dang. All right, how about if I . . . uh-oh. Better start thinking of an "official story" for the current state of my head.

I'd post a picture for you all, but I'm worried you might choke on your breakfast from laughing too hard, and, well, I don't want to be responsible for any mirth-related injuries. Suffice it to say, Amy has an, um, interesting birthday surprise waiting for her when she wakes up in the morning.

But remember, if anybody asks you, your response will be: "Gosh, Mike is so sweet—did you see that he shaved (most of?) his head in support of his poor, cancer-stricken wife?"

Got it? I knew I could count on you.

Oh, and adding insult to idiocy, I actually cut my ear shaving afterward.

I know, right? Life is rarely boring over here.

Love you all!

〜

At the time, I didn't know it would be Amy's last birthday on earth, and I loved hearing her laughter upstairs, even in the midst of her suffering. It was a tender mercy, both to me and to her, given freely from an unfailing God—a life-giving moment during a journey toward death.

The memory of that moment now makes me both smile and cry. I miss her laugh, her instant smile at the sight of my goofy head. I miss her more than I can even express. But I am glad that, on her final birthday, I did (accidentally) give her something that made her laugh.

PRAYER FOR TODAY

Lord God, surround me with Your tender mercies so I may live. And if You want to add a little laughter too, well, that'd be fine with me. Thank You!

Amen.

Yet I still belong to you; you hold my right hand. You guide me with your counsel, leading me to a glorious destiny.

PSALM 73:23–24 NLT

After you have suffered for a little while, the God of all grace, who called you to His eternal glory in Christ, will Himself perfect, confirm, strengthen and establish you.

1 PETER 5:10 NASB

There is surely a future hope for you, and your hope will not be cut off.

PROVERBS 23:18 NIV

To console those who mourn in Zion, to
give them beauty for ashes, the oil of joy
for mourning, the garment of praise for the
spirit of heaviness; that they may be called
trees of righteousness, the planting of the
LORD, that He may be glorified.

ISAIAH 61:3 NKJV

FIRST, YOU SHOULD KNOW SHE CALLS ME DUMPY
instead of Grandpa. It's a long story, but she's only four
years old. Amy had something to do with it too, so I like
that name because my two favorite girls gave it to me.

Second, she told me tonight that she misses her Mimi
(her name for Amy) and sometimes it makes her cry, like
when she was at dance class. When she was crying, her
dance teacher stopped the class to hug her, and she told me
that made her feel better. Then my granddaughter started
remembering for me the things she and her Mimi had
planned to do together.

"We never got to go on a boat ride," she said, "or fly an
airplane to somewhere special."

She stopped and tilted her head at me.

"Are you crying, Dumpy?" she asked.

I squeaked out, "Yes. I do that sometimes, just like you. It's OK to cry when you miss Mimi."

She looked at me for a moment. Then she got out of her chair, walked over, and hugged me tightly, and we both missed her Mimi together for a minute or two. Afterward I thought how Amy would be so sad to know her granddaughter is struggling with grief at such a young age.

But I think she would've liked that little hug. I think it would've made her smile through tears. Just like it did for me.

PRAYER FOR TODAY

Jesus, it is a strange thing to smile through tears. I may not be able to stop crying today, Lord. Will You help me find a reason to smile anyway?

Amen.

"He will wipe every tear from their eyes, and there will be no more death or sorrow or crying or pain. All these things are gone forever." And the one sitting on the throne said, "Look, I am making everything new!" And then he said to me, "Write this down, for what I tell you is trustworthy and true."

REVELATION 21:4–5 NLT

I HAVE A FOLDER ON MY COMPUTER WITH A BUNCH OF books I either wrote and couldn't get published or started writing and never finished. There are over one hundred books hidden in there.

Today I was looking for something in that folder and was surprised to find that in the summer of 2012, I wrote a picture book titled *I Told the Sun About Amy.*

It was supposed to be a book to help children express grief, with a gentle encouragement that God still cares even when we're sad. I put Amy's name in the title as a placeholder and then forgot to change it later.

The book was never published, and I'd forgotten most

of the story, so when I saw it today I was curious. I read *I Told the Sun About Amy* to myself. I took my time reading, trying to remember the images I'd originally envisioned when I decided to write the book.

It was a sad story (grief always is), and yes, I cried. Yet somehow when I finished the last page and dried the wet spots on my face, I realized something I hadn't expected. Reading a book that was meant to help children feel better helped me feel just a little bit better too. For a moment at least.

Now I'm sitting here and thinking. God is in the business of wiping away tears and making everything new. So I'm wondering if, four years ago, God planted that sweet, sad picture book manuscript in my mind, not for me to give to other children but for me to give to myself—just so I'd have it to read today, when I needed a way to feel better.

PRAYER FOR TODAY

Oh God, why do I cry (or feel like crying) so many times during the day? I long for You to wipe away my tears once and for all. Until then, help me trust in You.

Amen.

Yet what we suffer now is nothing compared
to the glory he will reveal to us later.

ROMANS 8:18 NLT

We can rejoice, too, when we run into problems and trials, for we know that they help us develop endurance. And endurance develops strength of character, and character strengthens our confident hope of salvation. And this hope will not lead to disappointment. For we know how dearly God loves us, because he has given us the Holy Spirit to fill our hearts with his love.

ROMANS 5:3–5 NLT

Christ himself is our peace.

EPHESIANS 2:14 NCV

WE WERE SITTING IN THE BASEMENT, WRAPPED UP IN blankets (because it's always chilly down there), watching something funny on TV. To Amy's left was the ubiquitous glass of iced tea that, over the years, had earned a seat of its own on the couch. I sat to her right, where it had been my job for nearly thirty years to scratch her back while our show was playing. While I scratched, she rested her hand on my leg, gently rubbing my aching muscles.

I see everything in this memory, the gray Captain America T-shirt of mine that she wore as her pajamas, the green Mickey Mouse pillows scattered nearby, the Red Vines on the counter. It's almost as if my mind took a photo and stored it in there while I wasn't looking.

And then, in between our binge-watching episodes, she turned to me.

"This feels like just a normal night," she said earnestly, "like I'm going to wake up tomorrow and find out that cancer was all just a bad dream."

She breathed. I waited. And then she leaned forward and rested her head on my knee.

"I don't want to die," she said quietly.

We were both crying now.

"I know," I said. I leaned over and wrapped my arms around her waist. She returned my embrace, and we were silent for a while. Finally, she kissed my face and smiled.

"It's going to be OK," she said, "no matter what happens." She leaned back into her seat. "Now turn on the next episode. I like feeling normal, even if it's just for tonight."

So we spent the rest of the evening being "normal." It was a strange island of peace within a long, difficult sea-journey from our married life to Amy's death. It was not just a night blown on mindless TV anymore. It had become a holy thing, a supernatural gift of kindness from the Spirit of Christ, wrapping us in His comfort, keeping us warmed by both His love and ours.

And two months later she was gone.

Now it is nearly a year since I've been forced to sit alone in that chilly little basement. I still can't watch new episodes of our show; I don't even record them anymore. It just feels awkward to watch without her. It doesn't feel normal.

I understand now what Amy felt that night, what she shared with me. It was the peace that settles over a life unhindered by worry or fear, blanketed in the strength and unity of a loving relationship. It is that sense of aware-ness of goodness, of well-being and security—of the Old Testament's *shalom* or the New Testament's *eirēnē*, or what we call peace. The certainty that *in spite of everything*, everything is going to be all right.[4]

That used to be "normal" for both Amy and me. An ordinary thing . . . but it is difficult to find that kind of peace without her sitting beside me, drinking iced tea, laughing at the imaginary world on our TV.

The apostle Paul tells me today that "Christ himself is our *eirēnē*." He is our peace. And I believe it in my mind. I've known that peace myself, intimately, though it seems like ages ago since I last saw it here in my life.

Christ, You are my peace. In my head I know this without question. But how long, oh Lord, must I wait before my lonely heart remembers it too?

PRAYER FOR TODAY

Lord Christ, You are my *eirēnē*. May Your supernatural peace rest in, on, and through me today. And especially tonight when I feel most alone.

Amen.

"The mountains may disappear, and the hills may come to an end, but my love will never disappear; my promise of peace will not come to an end," says the LORD who shows mercy to you.

ISAIAH 54:10 NCV

HOSPICE CARE IS AN AWFUL PLACE TO BE. DON'T GET ME wrong—everyone there is caring and compassionate and helpful. But everyone there also knows that death is the reason *you* are there, and that we all must talk about this death as if every moment isn't ripping through your soul like a serrated knife wielded by a sadist. And yet . . .

She loved me from that hospital bed.

Just as much, maybe more, than she ever had.

Who gets that, really, in this life? It is a rare and beautiful thing to have love that lasts a lifetime from a woman like Amy. As I reflect on her last weeks in hospice, I realize that living in that awful time broke me—and also gave me a few healing memories, priceless reminders of her love.

Once, we were sitting in her hospice room, not doing anything in particular, just waiting, and dying. She was thirsty, so I got up to get her some iced tea.

"I love you so much," she said to me suddenly, reaching for my hand from her hospital bed. "I feel like I'm not communicating how much I really love you." She was almost in tears. My heart was breaking. *I know how much you love me*, I wanted to say. But even more than that, I just wanted to see her smile at me again, that secret smile she hid from others and gave only to me.

"Honey," I grinned at her, holding her hand and looking deeply into her eyes.

And then I told her a slightly off-color joke, a private one where she was the star.

It was joy to hear her laugh, to see her smile at me again. And she knew that I knew how much she loved me. She kept my hand, lay back in bed, and smiled as she drifted off to sleep once more.

I returned to my chair, wondering what I'd ever done to deserve Amy's kind of love.

Ten days later she lapsed into a coma and spent the rest of her life mostly unresponsive, unable even to roll over or lift her head or open her lovely emerald eyes. During those last days, Amy and I were often alone in that hospice room.

One time, after the nurses had positioned Amy onto

her right side, there was space behind her on the bed. Suddenly I felt like I couldn't breathe anymore unless I could wrap my arms around her one last time. So I climbed in beside her, pressed my chest against her back, laid my head on her side, and just held her. And somewhere inside that coma, she knew I needed to hold her; she felt it.

Her shuttered eyes moistened, and she tried with great effort to turn toward me, to put her arms around me, but by that time she was much too weak to do more than shudder and tremble in my arms. I began to back away, hoping that would calm her, but she was inconsolable until I finally put my head under the crook of her arm, until the weight of her own weakness allowed her to cradle my head close to her heart. Only then did she settle back into the bed, breathe gently once more, and rest peacefully again.

I stayed that way a few minutes, loving her warmth next to me, worried that I was hurting her for my own selfish intimacy. And then, too soon, all the effort took its toll. She started writhing in pain, groaning, hurting. It took an hour of bolus (pain medicine) shots and some Ativan to finally ease her suffering. But even at the end, her heart was so tender toward me that she still wanted to comfort me when I was crushed beneath that moment, all those moments.

I felt sad that she suffered because of me, yet I now treasure those three minutes or so when she wrapped my head in her arm, when her love was adamant, unrelenting against all obstacles to reach for me. Even though she couldn't open her eyes, couldn't raise her head, could barely raise her arms, couldn't even roll on her back. Even though it was hurting her, she reached out to hold me as close as she possibly could.

I die again just remembering her little rabbit heartbeat in my ears.

I live again knowing that her love was mine, is mine, will be mine forever.

How, I've sometimes wondered, *could she love like that? So deeply, for so long?* But I know the answer.

Amy loved me fiercely because Jesus loved her the same way, all the way to the end. She gave to me love that she knew from experience, love described in Isaiah 54:

> "The mountains may disappear, and the hills may come to an end, but my love will never disappear . . . says the Lord."

PRAYER FOR TODAY

Jesus, I'm tired. I don't want to "do" anything today except rest and be loved by You. I know Your love will never disappear, that Your love is mine and will be mine forever. Thank You.

Amen.

So we do not lose heart. Though our outer self is wasting away, our inner self is being renewed day by day. For this light momentary affliction is preparing for us an eternal weight of glory beyond all comparison, as we look not to the things that are seen but to the things that are unseen. For the things that are seen are transient, but the things that are unseen are eternal.

2 CORINTHIANS 4:16–18 ESV

I DON'T EVEN REMEMBER WHY I HAD TO LEAVE—SOME list of unavoidable errands, I guess. I called a friend to come sit with Amy while I was gone, and when I came back to hospice, my body felt spent. Our friend left, and I sank down at the foot of Amy's hospital bed. We talked for a moment, and then I let myself wilt into the space next to her legs, my spine near her knee, the back of my head pressed lightly against her left hip.

"I'm exhausted," I mumbled. "Is it OK if I just lie here for a minute or two?"

I felt her gentle hand weave its fingers in my hair.

"Yes," she murmured. "Stay as long as you like."

We both closed our eyes. A moment later she was asleep, her hand still resting peacefully on my head.

I want to stay beside you forever, I thought.

Breath spilled quietly from her lungs; her fingers twitched lightly near my ear.

I want her to stay by me forever, I prayed. *Please God, let her stay.*

But sometimes God answers prayers in ways we don't want Him to, with things that are unseen.

PRAYER FOR TODAY

My Father, today I must remember that the things that are seen are transient, but the things that are unseen are eternal. Help me find hope in unseen things.

Amen.

> Lord, you alone are my portion and my cup;
> you make my lot secure. The boundary lines
> have fallen for me in pleasant places; surely I
> have a delightful inheritance.
>
> PSALM 16:5–6 NIV

From Amy's Journal—May 26, 2015
(Before Amy knew she had cancer)

‿

I know I tend to only journal when life is crappy—
so I wanted to memorialize the recent days as a
reminder that the majority of my life is great.

This past weekend Brianna graduated from
high school. So proud of her and her God-honoring
accomplishments. I hope she loves Mt. Hermon &
college. Seeing Anika cling to her and cry makes
me almost cry myself (actually I did cry a lot that
night).

Going to Comic Con with Mike on Saturday—

then Sunday going to graduation parties. And on Monday doing repair projects with Dad. Lunch and shopping with Mandi and Genevieve, seeing Tony & Zach, time to read and relax with Mike—and being there when G had her first ride on the train at North Lake Park and seeing her excitement . . .

LIFE IS GOOD!

These are the good old days. God is so good—I cannot even begin to describe His goodness!

ঙ

From Amy's Journal—May 26, 2016
*(Exactly one year later, after Amy learned
she would soon die from cancer)*

Last night was the first night at TCBY for the summer season. Everyone was there. Lots of laughing, stories, hugs. I got to give baby Cayde a taste of frozen yogurt—he was not impressed. And Genevieve gave lots of hugs and said, "I love my great-grandpa so much—and he loves me." So sweet.

These are the days of what life is.

AND—got a video message from James Taylor. Now how awesome is that!!??

I miss my girl, Lord. I miss her so much! But I'm beginning to see why she always quoted Psalm 16:5–6 at me. Amy was a gift to me, Your gift to me. Her steadfast joy, her authentic faith, her determined love—all of these things remind me even now that:

"The boundary lines have fallen for me in pleasant places; surely I have a delightful inheritance."

Thank You for Amy, Lord, for giving her to me as my delightful inheritance.

Amen.

PRAYER FOR TODAY

God, teach me to say like David, "The boundary lines have fallen for me in pleasant places . . . ."

Amen.

This suffering person cried out: the LORD listened and saved him from every trouble.

PSALM 34:6 CEB

Trust in the LORD with all your heart and lean not on your own understanding; in all your ways submit to him, and he will make your paths straight.

PROVERBS 3:5–6 NIV

For no one is abandoned by the LORD forever. Though he brings grief, he also shows compassion because of the greatness of his unfailing love. For he does not enjoy hurting people or causing them sorrow.

LAMENTATIONS 3:31–33 NLT

> Rejoice with those who rejoice, weep with
> those who weep.
>
> ROMANS 12:15 ESV

JEFF HAS CALLED ME. I'M TERRIFIED.

It's been six weeks since his wife died, and our friends have told him to come see me about it. It's like they think we're supposed to start a club or something.

So, what am I supposed to do now, Lord?

How is the sick man supposed to pretend to be a doctor?

I can't find healing for my own soul, even after all these months. What will I say to Jeff that will miraculously bring to him the healing I myself am unable to accomplish? I am woefully inadequate. Losing Amy didn't magically make me a grief counselor, did it?

I can't do it. I'm going to cancel our meeting . . .

But how can I do that to Jeff?

How can I live with my own regret if I, knowingly, let him suffer this agony alone?

Oh Jesus, why is grief such a complicated, hurtful thing?

My friend Danny is telling me, "Weep with those who weep, brother. Weep with those who weep." He speaks from experience. After all, isn't that what he did with me not so long ago, even though my sorrow came only two years after his own wife had died?

All right.

I know how to weep. I've been crying nonstop since September 11, 2016. I'm good at it. All day, every day, is just a series of hours while I'm holding back my tears. (I should become an actor because now I can cry on command.)

I can't solve Jeff's problems. I can't heal Jeff's pain. But maybe what he needs is just someone to be sick with him, someone to sit next to him who will cry and curse while he cries and curses.

OK, I'll do it. I'll go to Jeff and listen, and do what Danny did for me, do what Jesus still does:

Weep with those who weep.

PRAYER FOR TODAY

Lord Jesus, I am now very good at weeping (as You already know). Help me, then, to be someone who weeps with those who weep— just like You always do with me.

Amen.

Brothers and sisters, we want you to know about those Christians who have died so you will not be sad, as others who have no hope. We believe that Jesus died and that he rose again. So, because of him, God will raise with Jesus those who have died. . . . So encourage each other with these words.

1 THESSALONIANS 4:13–14, 18 NCV

LETTER TO AMY

September 07, 2016

Dear Amy,

I'm sitting here watching you struggle to breathe, hearing the nurse and the doctor say you will die soon, surprised that I have any more tears left within me, wishing I could do something, anything to make you happy one more time.

I loved making you happy. It made me happier than even I could have imagined.

And yet, here we are. So even though I know you will never read this, even though I know you already know this (we've talked about these things a thousand times!), I want to write it all down so that someday, when I'm better, when I'm mostly whole again, I can read it to myself and remember you, and smile.

I want to say thank you. You've made my life worth living, and that's saying a lot for me because

I've never been crazy about this awful planet and these frail bodies we are forced to inhabit.

Thank you for making me feel safe. When you were near, nothing could hurt me, not for long at least. Today I made your hand wipe away my tears. You have always been so good at that, and it devastates me that you'll no longer be able to do this for me. But for thirty years, I knew what it felt like to be safe, because of you.

Thank you for loving me fiercely, with loyalty that borders on the supernatural. Thank you for telling me you loved me first thing every morning before you got out of bed, for telling me again every night just before you drifted off to sleep, and for telling me a dozen times in between during the day.

I learned from you that the greatest part of love is loyalty. You always were determined to build me up, never to tear me down. You never insulted me, or put me down, or belittled me in order to show yourself superior (even though you are superior in so many ways). You never let me be embarrassed in front of others, never told humorously insulting stories about me to our friends without my permission, never reprimanded me in front of others, at least not in ways they'd see.

You always stood up for me when others told jokes at my expense or tried to say anything about me that was hurtful or unkind. You stood between me and many pains. So thank you for that fierce, loyal love. It is irreplaceable.

Thank you for liking me as much as you loved me, for always being my errand buddy, for standing in line with me/for me at Comic Cons, for taking vacation time from work just to go see movies nominated for Academy Awards with me. Thank you for sleeping next to me on the couch while I watched football, for just sitting in the same room while we both read books, for holding my hand in soapy dishwater, for being better than a best friend.

When I was with you, next to you, that was the only place in my world where I felt like I truly belonged, where I could finally relax and just be at peace. I loved belonging to you. Your open arms made me safe. Gave me healing. Protected my soul. Thank you.

Thank you for sharing your dreams with me, and not being mad at me when I pushed you to make those dreams a reality, even though they scared you, even when you didn't think they were possible. (And I'm sorry I didn't take you to see

James Taylor when he was in Denver . . . twice. I just thought we'd have more time! Thank you for forgiving me that selfish failure.)

Thank you for always smiling when I came into a room.

Thank you for letting me make you happy. I don't know what to do with myself now, because that's all I ever wanted to do, just make you happy. Thank you for being happy with me.

Thank you for listening to gospel music with me on Sunday mornings.

Thank you for making Lebanese food for me every birthday and Christmas.

Thank you for making wonderful family traditions and fantastic family memories. For always setting up the Christmas tree and just letting me watch your beauty while you hung our ornaments— every ornament with its own story.

Thank you for so, so, so much laughter.

Thank you for holding my hand under the covers while we watched movies or TV shows in our freezing basement.

Thank you for holding my hand when we walked from the car, through the parking lot, into the store.

Thank you for holding my hand while you

slept, while you were dying, for reaching for my hand when you knew I was crying, for trying to hug me when you couldn't even lift your head.

Thank you for this agony I feel right now, watching your labored last breaths, suffering through these last moments while you are still warm. It means I have loved you deeply, loved you because you taught me how to love. I hate this moment, hate this day, hate the sun callously shining right outside this hospital window. But I'm grateful that it is *your* love that brought me here.

Thank you, my girl. Thank you so much. For everything. For all, and forever.

I love you, fiercely, back.
MIKEY

AFTERWORD

THIS MONTH MARKS THE SIXTH ANNIVERSARY OF THE
day that Amy died. It also happens to be the time when
I'm finalizing the manuscript of this book for you. That's
probably not coincidence, right?

With that in mind, six years later, I felt Jesus whispering in my ears words I didn't fully understand but with an
intention I couldn't mistake. So I have a few last things I'd
like to say to you, my friend, if you have time.

1. I'm Sorry.

When people ask me what this book is about, I tell them:
It's not about helping you get over grief. It's about simply
helping you to grieve, giving you time to mourn. Someone
to weep with. A safe space to feel what's necessary, but
often unwelcome, after the funeral. Others usually don't
understand that. They want me to give you "Seven Steps
to Conquering Grief" or "29 Prayers to Make Grief Go
Away" or other silly things like that.

But you get it, I think. You understand. Otherwise you wouldn't be here with me right now. And I'm sorry that you've known the kind of pain that makes you understand.

My wife, when she was dying, used to tell me, "Mikey, the only way you're going to *get* through this is to *go* through it." And she was right. So I know and want to acknowledge that, even though you've reached the end of this book, that doesn't mean you've miraculously overcome your sorrow. That you no longer miss your loved one.

There are no words that can ever fill the place that precious person held in your heart, not enough paper and ink on the planet to make up for what you've lost. This life is hard sometimes, and it pains me that you and I have had to share this experience of such heartbreaking loss. So, again, all I really know to say to you is:

I'm so, so sorry.

2. About Sorrow and Joy

I also want you to know something I was surprised to discover: Joy and sorrow are not mutually exclusive. Feeling one does not erase the other, or at least it doesn't have to.

Have you ever read the Gospel accounts about the night before Christ's crucifixion? During the last meal with His disciples, Jesus said, "I have told you these things so that *you will be filled with my joy*" (John 15:11 NLT, italics mine). Immediately after dinner, He took His disciples to the garden at Gethsemane and told them, "My soul is *crushed with grief* to the point of death" (Matthew 26:38 NLT, italics mine).

God incarnate, in the same hour on the same night, is both filled with joy and crushed with grief. This is why it's true that Jesus can be our "man of sorrows" (Isaiah 53:3) while at the same time His Spirit constantly bears the fruit of joy in our lives (Galatians 5:22).

So when you next find yourself filled with sorrow— today, tomorrow, ten minutes from now, six months from now—I encourage you not to deny it or push it down or disown it. Rather, do what Jesus did: accept it, acknowledge it . . . but don't let that sorrow prevent you from also feeling, and pursuing, honest joy. One emotion does not have to exclude the other. You can feel sad—and still take pride in your work; you can ache with longing for your loved one—and also enjoy a night out with friends and family.

I remember one time, only a few months after Amy had passed, I was playing with my granddaughter. As we laughed at the Jenga tower falling over, I remember being delighted by her smile—and also feeling great sadness because I saw Amy reflected in Gigi's emerald eyes. Both emotions were right and good and appropriate for the time—as they can be for you. So don't let sorrow prevent you from making the most of each day God gives to you;

joy is part of your birthright as His child, and it's the Holy Spirit's gift to you in even the worst of circumstances.

Joy and sorrow, mixed together, make a special kind of wine with a sweetness all its own. Others won't get to taste that; they simply don't have the means. But now, today, you do. Please allow yourself to drink from that cup whenever you feel it's necessary.

3. The Suicide Thing

During that first year after Amy died, people who didn't know me well were always worried I might commit suicide. When I'd speak of Amy resting in heaven and how I longed to one day be with her there, they'd get all panicky and stressed and start reciting reasons to live and recommending good counselors and lecturing me on the richness of life. They didn't get it. Longing for heaven doesn't mean I'm craving self-harm any more than loving pizza means I hate tacos (which I don't!). It just means I have something very precious to look forward to when this life is finally done for me.

Still, I can't avoid the fact that maybe you've thought about taking matters into your own hands, contemplating an abrupt end to what may feel to you is a miserable existence right now. So, I'm going to tell you the same things I tell my friends who fret with worry over my life:

When Christ welcomed my girl into His arms, I'm

fairly certain He didn't grimace and say, "Oh crap! I forgot to get Mike!"

That means, as long as there is breath in my body, there is purpose to my life. It's His breath and His purpose in me, for as long as He wants, however He wants it. In the end, though I miss Amy with every heartbeat, Christ alone is my reason for living—not her. As Paul explained to the people of Athens, "*In him* we live and move and have our being" (Acts 17:28 NIV, italics mine).

Also, despite what well-meaning people preach at me, I must remember that God didn't prolong my life in order for me to accomplish some great task! My existence doesn't depend on what I *accomplish*, only on who I *become*.

Romans 8:29 tells me I live so that God can shape me into a person like His Son. That's all my life needs to be about, and it's enough. Apparently Amy was just better at that growing-to-be-like-Jesus thing than I am, and she was able to finish sooner. So I must be patient and trust that He who began a good work in me will be faithful to complete it—in *His* good time, not in mine (Philippians 1:6).

Now, dear friend, please understand this: what's true for me is also true for you. *You are not here by accident.*

Your pain is not enough to extinguish God's work in your soul. Don't insult yourself, and God, by pushing aside His ever-active purpose for you. And, of course, if you need help, please ask for it. Your local community likely has crisis counselors available, but if not, you can always use one of these resources:

Call the National Suicide Prevention Hotline: 1-800-273-8255.

Text "Hello" to 741741 to start a texting dialogue with someone at the Crisis Text Hotline.

Dial or text 988, which is the three-digit, nationwide phone number to connect directly to the 988 Suicide and Crisis Lifeline.

All right, I guess that's enough for now.

Thank you for walking with me, for a time, in the valley of the shadow of death. And thank you for the great honor of letting me walk next to you. My prayer at the end of this book is the same as our prayer at the beginning:

May God help us both to grieve well—to the fullest, to the utmost, into the arms of Jesus. Amen.

MIKEY

September 2022

NOTES

1. J. D. Douglas, ed., *The Illustrated Bible Dictionary,
   Part 1: Aaron–Golan* (Leicester, England: Inter-Varsity
   Press, 1980), 201.
2. R. T. Kendall, *The Sermon on the Mount* (Minneapolis,
   MN: Chosen Books, 2011), 22.
3. See King David's introductory notes, included as part of
   the text of Psalm 34.
4. Lawrence O. Richards, *The Revell Bible Dictionary,
   Deluxe Color Edition* (Old Tappan, NJ: Fleming H.
   Revell Company, 1980), 766.

BIBLE TRANSLATIONS

Scripture quotations marked CEB are taken from the Common English Bible. Copyright © 2011 Common English Bible. Visit www.CommonEnglishBible.com.

Scripture quotations marked CEV are taken from the Contemporary English Version. Copyright © 1991, 1992, 1995 by American Bible Society. Used by permission.

Scripture quotations marked ESV are taken from the ESV® Bible (The Holy Bible, English Standard Version®). Copyright © 2001 by Crossway, a publishing ministry of Good News Publishers. Used by permission. All rights reserved.

Scripture quotations marked HCSB are taken from the Holman Christian Standard Bible®. Copyright © 1999, 2000, 2002, 2003, 2009 by Holman Bible Publishers. Used by permission. HCSB® is a federally registered trademark of Holman Bible Publishers.

Scripture quotations marked NASB are taken from the New American Standard Bible®. Copyright © 1960, 1962,

ABOUT THE AUTHOR

MIKE NAPPA IS A BESTSELLING AND AWARD-WINNING author with millions of copies of his books sold worldwide. An Arab-American and practical theologian, Mikey holds an MA in Bible and Theology, an MA in English, and a BA in Christian Education. He writes about the Bible and Christian life for Crosswalk.com, Christianity.com, Beliefnet.com, and others. Plus he collects Captain America comics so, you know, he's got that going for him.